M000078207

THE ME FACTOR

YOUR SYSTEMATIC GUIDE TO
GETTING WHAT THE HELL YOU WANT

DR. GANZ FERRANCE
Registered Psychologist

Advance Praise for *The Me Factor*

"I've read literally hundreds of books about personal and professional excellence and development, and not one has resonated with the truth, reality, and practicality of *The Me Factor*. Read the damn book."

—Chris Venn,
Entrepreneur

"I'm talking straight to the men here… As high performers, we want to do and give our best. But you can't give and do your best if you don't feel your best. You may be burnt-out, stressed-out, pissed off, or just tired. Dr. Ganz gives you a down-to-earth, easy-to-read guide that puts you back into the driver's seat of your own life."

—Joseph Ranseth,
Speaker and #1 International Bestselling Author of
Go Ahead, Start A Movement

"A must-read if you care about the men in your life. Finally, a practical step-by-step way to help those you love to find a way to win. I see too many who sacrifice themselves, developing serious, life-threatening health challenges due to chasing success in their professional lives. Thank you, Dr. Ganz, for bringing forward this program. I am going to share it with many and often."

—Tamara Hunter,
Executive Director and Cofounder of
Chemo Buddies for Life

"Thank you, Dr. Ganz, for writing a book for MEN! ***The Me Factor*** system clearly shows the way to success for men who want to get the best out of life—not just success at work, but in their lives. I will be recommending this book to not only all of my male clients who are struggling with stress and burnout, but to their loved ones as well."

—Dianne Ansari-Winn, MD, MPH
Founder of ***Physician Vitality Institute***

"***The Me Factor*** is an important book for men because it offers a roadmap for changing the way we work, live, and serve. Without the guidance that Dr. Ganz delivers, too many men will keep burning themselves out and not be able to accomplish the great things they want in this lifetime for the benefit of the world."

—Ben Gioia,
Creator of ***InfluenceWithAHeart.com***
and President of ***Leadership Awake, LLC***

"Simply brilliant! Where was this book thirty years ago when I needed it? ***The Me Factor*** is a powerful yet light look at why we overachievers in the world 'push until it's too late!' This may be one of the most important books you ever buy."

—Teresa de Grosbois
#1 International Bestselling Author of
Mass Influence - Habits of the Highly Influential

"A ground-breaking book that is long overdue! Tapping into the hearts and minds of workaholics who have lost their zest for life. They work day and night only to lose sight of their identities—who they are, what they want, and where they would like to go. It is time for men to realize they cannot serve others and get the results they want if they cannot take care of themselves. This book is a must-read for the man in your life!"

—Debra Kasowski,
Award-Winning Bestselling Author,
Speaker, Trainer, & Coach, **www.debrakasowski.com**

"Dr. Ganz has written a personal and professional masterpiece with his innovative book, ***The Me Factor***. This new approach for men allows the reader to learn and understand their life's purpose. Ultimately, it's about being empowered to take charge of your life on every level. Dr. Ganz guides you every step of the way. ***The Me Factor*** is educational, positive, and inspirational, with an honest look at the lives of men in the 21st century. This book should also be read by mothers, women, and wives to help them better understand the male psyche, and to understand and see any male counterpart with new eyes. Men deserve respect, and Dr. Ganz shows us the how, the why, and the easy steps to take to succeed in life."

—Gary Stuart,
Author, ***Master YOUR Universe,***
Constellation Facilitator

"Dr. Ganz offers a way forward for men to embrace workaholism in its correct and more pleasing contribution to life."

—Dr. Stephen Hobbs,
Founder, ***WELLth Movement***

"As a leadership expert who works in the corporate space and with many men in business, I highly recommend Dr. Ganz Ferrance's book ***The Me Factor***. It is a resource every man should have in his toolkit. In this powerful book, Dr. Ferrance guides men through a process of discovery to better understand the biggest obstacles and challenges they often face and how all their effort has, in many cases, been misplaced or has come at the cost of their own well-being. This book is designed to help men gain clarity about what they truly want, take back their own personal power, and discover how to put the ladder of success against the right wall to open up greater abundance, wellness, peace, and joy for themselves. A must-read for any man wanting a deeper, richer, and more fulfilling life!"

—Candy Barone,
International Speaker, Amazon Bestselling Author,
CEO & Founder of **You Empowered Strong (Y.E.S.), LLC**

"***The Me Factor*** is a fresh look from a man's point of view, written for and to men who are functioning workaholics to make themselves a priority and to help them start living a life they love."

—Charmaine Hammond,
Professional Speaker and Bestselling Author

"If work equals play, then you can play all the time. If work equals work, and you work hard, then you burn yourself out. Yikes! In ***The Me Factor***, Dr. Ganz paints a framework (with a number of AHAs) for men who are overworked. In this book, he shares the formula that worked for him and is designed for you to engineer your own 'personal maintenance' to drive a positive impact in both your personal and professional life. If you want to find balance, if you want people to feel your authenticity and truly know, like, and trust you, then read this book."

—Mitchell Levy,
The AHA Guy at ***AHAthat*** *and TED Speaker,*
http://aha.pub/TEDtalk

Copyright © 2018 Dr. Ganz Ferrance

All rights reserved. The scanning, uploading, and electronic sharing of any part of this book without the permission of the publisher is unlawful piracy and theft of the author's intellectual property. Please purchase only authorized editions, and do not participate in or encourage electronic piracy of copyrighted materials. If you would like to use material from this book (other than for review purposes), prior written permission must be obtained by contacting the author at info@DoctorGanz.com

Thank you for your support of this author's rights.

Legal and Medical Disclaimers: Although Dr. Ganz Ferrance is a Registered Psychologist, this book is a work of his own opinions and not necessarily guaranteed facts. Many of these opinions are backed by statistics, research, and decades of clinical experience. However, this book has been written for entertainment purposes and should not be viewed in any other manner. Even though there are many resources in this book, there is no obligation to accept the ideas and opinions expressed by the author or go against your own judgment. Please consult your own physicians, psychologists, religious leaders, etc.… and form your own opinions.

Although the author has made every effort to ensure that the information in this book is correct at time of press, the author does not assume and does hereby disclaim any liability to any party for any loss, damage, or disruption caused by errors or omissions, whether such errors or omissions result from negligence, accident or any other issue.

This book is not intended to be a substitute for the advice of a mental health or other professional. The reader should regularly consult qualified professionals in all matters relating to his/her mental, emotional or physical health and/or the mental, emotional or physical health of their child/children and particularly with respect to any symptoms that may require diagnosis or medical attention. The information in this book is meant to supplement, not replace, proper counseling and/or guidance and/or medical and/or legal advice.

Editor: Front Rowe Seat Communications, karen@karenrowe.com

Cover Design: Shake Creative, Shake Tampa.com

Inside Layout: Ljiljana Pavkov

Printed in Canada

FIRST EDITION

ISBN: 978-0-9959858-0-3 (paperback)

ISBN: 978-0-9959858-1-0 (ebook)

Published by The Ferrance Group

To my wife Dyan and my kids, Ayanna and Ganz Jr., for putting up with me and helping me be a better person.

"Know thyself."
– *Ancient aphorism*

Table of Contents

THE ME FACTOR

Preface

Imagine you wake up one morning to the sound of your alarm clock. You roll over, hit the snooze button, roll back again, look up at the ceiling...and realize you don't know where the hell you are.

Your body feels heavy and warm. You don't recognize the room. You don't remember going to bed the night before. You have no idea how you got here. You look around for any kind of reminder, but nothing seems familiar.

This is exactly what happened to me one morning as a young man. For several minutes, all I did was lie there, very confused and getting more worried by the minute. I truly thought I was having a stroke.

Finally, it hits me. I'm in Lac La Biche, a little town in northern Alberta, Canada. It's Tuesday, and I have to go to work. I get up and go through the regular motions, but the moments of that morning linger with me for the rest of the day. I can't ignore it any longer. I am a workaholic. I had not been taking care of myself, I am completely burned out, and it is starting to show up in scary ways.

I stopped reading fairy tales and fables long ago, but one that stuck with me through the years was Aesop's fable "The Goose that Laid the Golden Egg": A poor farmer was so destitute he could barely support his family. All he had was a goose whose eggs he would take to market and sell in order to buy other supplies for his family. One day, he found his goose had laid a golden egg. He was amazed. He took the egg to a merchant in town who confirmed that the egg was indeed real and solid gold.

Of course, as the story goes, the goose continued to lay golden eggs, and the farmer eventually became so wealthy that he had more money than he knew what to do with. Every day, he would check his goose and find another solid gold egg—but only one. Along with the new wealth, the farmer became more impatient and conceited. Why did the goose only lay one egg at a time? Imagine the riches he could have if it would lay half a dozen a day! So one day, in a fit of impatience, he grabbed the goose by the neck and cut it open to get all the golden eggs. Of course, he found nothing but goose guts. He had just killed the goose that laid the golden egg!

The morning when I woke up in Lac La Biche and didn't know where I was, I came to a life-changing realization. My lifestyle as a workaholic was not only harming myself but also sabotaging my own hard work. I was killing my own golden goose.

I was fresh out of university, with a PhD in Psychology. I had quickly connected with a prominent psychologist in Edmonton who had gotten me a job with a work schedule that was grueling, to say the least. I would leave my house in Bonnyville every Monday morning at 5 a.m. to pick up another psychologist who lived an hour and a half away. Together, we'd drive for another three hours to Fort McMurray. There, I'd pick up a social worker and drive another one and a half to two hours to Conklin. Once we arrived in Conklin, my workday finally began.

I would arrive at work around 11:00 a.m. and work until 6:00 p.m. When my work was done, I would drive back to Fort McMurray, drop off the social worker, get something to eat, then I'd go to the hotel.

I did this four days a week. I was driving a minimum of four hours daily—sometimes five—and eating my lunch in the car. I would see clients all day and supervise in-home care workers in the evenings.

I had never worked so hard in my life, but I wanted to prove myself. I'd been raised on the good, old-fashioned Protestant work ethic: hard work was healthy. And the harder the work, the greater the reward, right?

Every day was a struggle just to hold on, but I kept at it. Six months in, I began experiencing daily headaches. It was actually one lingering headache that never went away. I started taking medication to ease the pain; but instead of taking sick days or time off, I just kept working. I kept pushing myself.

Two weeks later, I woke up in that motel in Lac La Biche and didn't recognize the motel, didn't know where I was, and couldn't remember what town I was in. Once I realized where I was, I called the clinic and cancelled all my appointments for the day. It was the first time I realized I wasn't invincible to the effects of stress and deprivation, that there were physical, mental, and psychological consequences from overworking yourself like this. In my quest for greater and greater rewards, I had cut open my own goose. And what did I have to show for it? Goose guts.

When you look at the worldwide average of work hours per week, ranked by nation, the United States comes in second. Japan tops the list. Perhaps it's no surprise that the Japanese have a word, *karoshi*, that means "overwork death." Death by work is such a common part of their culture that it requires its own word.

For men—particularly family men in our thirties and forties—there is a major push for us to seek all of our golden eggs at once, as fast as we possibly can. There may not be an English word for "overwork death," but make no mistake, working yourself to death is definitely a theme of our culture. From an early age, we're brought up to be like that farmer—impatient to the point of self-destruction. When we start to burn out, we soldier on. We push ourselves even harder. As a result, most men kill their goose, and themselves, without even knowing they're doing it.

This problem is endemic in our culture, and it needs to stop. That's why I developed the Me Factor System. This is a personal maintenance system which I will outline in detail in the coming chapters.

In this book, you will learn that working yourself to death is not a prerequisite for happiness and abundance. You will learn to work *with* the laws of the universe and the physical laws of the human body, rather than working against them. This is the essence of "feeding the goose."

By understanding and implementing certain Me Factors, you can live your life richly and go further, faster and easier.

My philosophy is, why work harder when you can work smarter? Do it the easy way. Use the Me Factor principles. Follow the steps in this book, and you can live to enjoy the rewards of your labor with your vitality and happiness intact.

Let's make sure those golden eggs never disappear.

Acknowledgments:

I would like to thank the following:

My clients for teaching me so much.

Karen Rowe and her team at Front Rowe Seat for organizing my thoughts and getting me over the finish line. Thank you for your amazing dedication, care and support during this whole project.

Maria Orydzuk for being my "muse."

Dr. Ed Joseph and Dr. Lynne Zettl for being my psychologists and keeping me "sane".

Kojenwa Moitt and her crew at Zebra PR for helping me stay organized and getting the word out.

Teresa de Grosbois and the Evolutionary Business Council for encouraging me to play a much bigger game.

My mother and the rest of the clan for being my inspiration.

Introduction

Most people spend their whole lives climbing the ladder of success only to realize, when they get to the top, the ladder has been leaning against the wrong wall.

– Stephen Covey

My name is Ganz Ferrance. I have a PhD in Counseling Psychology and an MA in Developmental Psychology from Andrews University in Michigan. I'm the former Public Education Coordinator and Vice President of the Psychologists' Association of Alberta. However, more important than all of that, I am a man, like you, who lives with high expectations and social pressure to perform. To work hard. To give 110 percent in everything we do, at all times.

In other words, to kill ourselves.

I've been a practicing psychologist for over twenty-five years, and I spend my time helping individuals, couples, families, and corporations reduce their stress, improve their relationships, and enjoy success in their professional and personal lives.

Psychology is a very broad field, but we therapists are trained in how the mind works and how to help people have stronger relationships and understand better how they think and how their feelings interact with and impact their behaviors.

Essentially, my job is to help people feel, do, and be better. That is my goal in this book: to help you *feel better, do better, and be better* in your life through the Me Factor System, a personal maintenance program that literally saved my life.

I've met so many overworked men who simply don't know they are depleting themselves. The worst part is, many of them have never stopped to ask why. "Why am I doing this? What is the point of it all?"

As men, we are susceptible to doing things simply because we think it's what we're supposed to be doing. Many men operate this way for decades. Then they turn forty or fifty, or they have a health crisis, or they get divorced, or the kids leave home, or something drastic happens, and they have to take stock of their lives. This is when they are forced to reevaluate and suddenly realize, per Stephen Covey's quote above, that they've climbed the ladder of success, and it's been leaning against the wrong wall the whole time.

If you are reading this book, chances are you are burned out, miserable, tired, resentful, and pissed off, and you don't understand why. Maybe you have health problems that seem to have come out of nowhere. This is because we tend to neglect ourselves, usually without ever realizing it. With a job, a spouse, and maybe a couple of kids, personal maintenance gets pushed to the back burner.

We don't intentionally neglect ourselves: it just happens. And over time, we pay the price. Personal maintenance, by default, is low on our list of priorities. The Me Factor System rectifies that by putting *you* at the center of your own life. You make *you* your top priority.

A "me-first" philosophy is difficult for many of us to accept. It flies in the face of our culture's idealization of selflessness and humility. But you'll soon learn that the more energy and abundance you pour into *yourself*, the more there is to overflow to the other areas of your life.

There have been times in my life when I've been swept along by the current, neglected my own personal maintenance, and suffered as a result. We all need a set of guidelines to make sure this doesn't happen, and the first step is to determine what we need, not just physically but emotionally, intellectually, spiritually, and socially.

What's missing from your life? What's important to you? Too many people have never taken the time to ask themselves those questions.

When a man doesn't know what is important to him, his decisions are made based on whatever is *urgent* at the time—whoever is currently the most pissed off with him, whatever pressing matter cannot be ignored a single second longer, or whatever will provide the most immediate benefit. Driving that decision-making process, often at an unconscious level, is the compulsion to do the "right thing," based on the expectations of culture, religion, or family.

The average man never really thinks about what he wants, what's good for him, what would make him happy, or what is going to serve the biggest part of his life in the best way.

My purpose in writing this book is to show you that you can choose to fill yourself up, discover what works for you, and serve others from a place of prosperity and abundance in a way that doesn't deplete you.

The Me Factor System has three parts:

1. The Me Factor Priority Schematic
2. The Me Factor Owner's Manual
3. The Decision Matrix

First, we will examine the often unspoken challenges of being a man. We'll shine a light on the personal and professional pressures faced by working men in our thirties and forties, when work and family pressures tend to be at their highest. You'll learn how to prioritize the areas of your life in a healthy way, create boundaries, and become a wellspring of energy that overflows into every area of your life.

We'll discuss each of The Seven Me Factors in detail—what they mean, why they matter, and how to cultivate them—and teach you how to fill out your own Me Factor Owner's Manual. Finally, we'll bring it all together with The Decision Matrix so you can start getting what the hell you want, now.

Be forewarned: this book is going to make you uncomfortable at times. I am going to ask you to get outside your comfort zone. You'll have to learn to be comfortable being uncomfortable, or at least as comfortable as possible. As the famous Henry Ford aphorism goes, if you continue doing what you've always done, you'll continue getting what you always got.

For many years, I didn't think I had anything to share. But I wouldn't be writing this book if the strategies didn't work. I wouldn't be walking my clients through this program, hosting workshops or making TV appearances to share this system if I didn't feel like there was something extraordinary here.

In the following chapters, we will look at what is preventing you from making the changes you need to make in your life, and I will give you concrete steps to improve your personal maintenance. If you are tired and burned out, keep reading.

Chapter One

Take a Break Already! Our Ongoing Battle with Burnout

When I was in the United States in the 1990s, I remember reading an article about an outfit in New York City, near Wall Street, that started an adult day care center. But this was not the kind of adult day care where you might take an elderly parent. It was designed for high-ranking businesspeople who needed a break. That's right: day care for executives.

Powerful, wealthy businessmen and women would go to this day care center and ride adult-sized tricycles and play with big blocks. They had juice and cookies and even nap time. These stressed-out executives, with the weight of the world and immense responsibilities on their shoulders, could play and be little kids. What they found was that it made them much sharper. They were able to return to work and be far more productive because they gave their minds a break.

This is an example of the ridiculous extent we are willing to go to get relief from burnout. What if, instead, we could avoid burnout entirely? What if you could exponentially increase your output without sacrificing your well-being in the process?

The good news is, you can. It all comes down to personal maintenance and a little planning.

In my Preface, I took you back to nursery school—to The Goose that Laid the Golden Egg. Who or what do you most identify with in that story? Are you the impatient farmer? The hapless goose? The priceless egg?

The truth is, you are really all three.

You Are the Golden Egg

You produce results on a daily basis. You work hard to provide for your family. You bring in money, and you put food on the table. What you do and who you are is as valuable as a golden egg, and as long as you can keep working—as long as you keep having results—the eggs keep coming.

You Are the Goose

You, as a person, are the source of your results. You produce those golden eggs. No one else will look after your family the way you do. No one else will build your business. Without you, no one will run community services or volunteer activities the way you can. If some foolish farmer were to suddenly kill you in a fit of impatience, it would place a permanent halt on production. No one produces the golden eggs in your life if you're not there.

You Are the Farmer

You care for the goose. You are in charge of its health and well-being, which in turn affects the quality of the rewards it provides. The better you care for it, the bigger your daily egg. You both create and receive the benefits of the golden egg.

I don't know about you, but if I had a goose that laid a golden egg every day, I would build her a little goose resort. I would feed her only the very best "goose chow." I would make sure she had some goose friends to keep her company, and I'd make sure she was healthy, happy, and lived a very, very long life. I wouldn't want to stress her out. I wouldn't want to demand more of her than she could handle. I wouldn't want to neglect giving her the care she needed if she was sick or suffering—*years* of golden eggs could hang in the balance! I would do everything I could to ensure my own prosperity by making sure she was well taken care of.

This all seems pretty logical, right? The problem is, men fail to see that the very same rewards—and consequences—are at stake in our lives every day. We should care for ourselves as we would for a magical source of gold.

Welcome Aboard Your Private Jet

A word about the "systematic" nature of things: If you don't understand how something is put together and how it works, you don't stand a chance in hell at looking after it effectively, much less getting the most out of it. We were never taught how our brain works or how our life is put together. You need this information to help you make the changes outlined in The Me Factor. You need this information to grow your life and make other changes that move you forward. Here's the analogy that helps me:

Let's say you just inherited a new, ultra-high-tech jet, complete with the latest artificial intelligence program. This jet is so advanced that it actually flies itself. You can still go into the cockpit and run things yourself if you feel like it, but it will always automatically adjust and get back on course once you let go of the stick. This jet also has the ability to learn from how you fly it and where you go. Your new jet comes pre-programmed with certain destinations, so once it's in the air it will automatically take you to those destinations. The only way to change where you go is to "teach" it where you want to go by manually flying there enough times that the AI program finally gets the message and accepts this as a new destination.

This is actually how your brain works. Your unconscious or subconscious mind is the autopilot; your conscious mind (what we think of as our "will" and freedom of choice) is you choosing a destination and taking control of the stick. The pre-programmed destinations are your core beliefs and unconscious habits (physical as well as emotional and mental). Your core beliefs and unconscious habits were "pre-programmed" pretty early on by the home you grew up in, your school, church, the media, and society in general. They were also influenced by your early experiences and how long and how often you followed those patterns (flew to those destinations).

Here's the deal: all the stuff you're learning/going to learn in this book is probably way different than how you're used to thinking about things. Making these (or any) changes in your life happens much more easily if you understand how things are set up and if you work with that system instead of fighting against it or working at random. You can constantly fight with the controls in the cockpit whenever you notice that you're "off course" – but as soon as you get tired, fall asleep, or have to go pee, you let go of the stick and the autopilot takes you right back to the original heading and you have to start all over again or end up where you don't want to be. (By the way, most people don't actually notice that they are off course until long after they land and get off the plane. Then they look around and say, "How the hell did I end up here –AGAIN!!?" This is what "self-sabotage" and being "your own worst enemy" looks like.) For most people any positive gains are made by chance at best, and at worst people have a hard struggle in life if their "pre-programming" is negative.

This is why change and personal growth can seem so frustrating that people give up and just resign themselves to running out the clock on their lives, never reaching their potential or experiencing the success and happiness they crave. A better way is to be systematic about things. You will have to put in the time to make the lasting changes (reprogram the autopilot/your subconscious). So build a plan and use ALL the tools, resources and support that will help you accomplish this (like the ones in this book and others at **TheMeFactor.me**). But once that's accomplished you will now go to the new (better) destination without much effort on your part. All the work is in the front end – but it's totally worth it.

Understand that every time you do things in the old way you're reinforcing the old programming. But when you can practice the new way of thinking, feeling, doing and being, you are training the autopilot to take you to that better place in your life that has all the stuff you really want.

Of course, in order to have the energy to reprogram your jet you have to fill the "Me circle/tank.". This is yet another reason that you need to work the Me Factor system. As all of us know, when you're hungry, angry, lonely, tired, (HALT), or otherwise out of your optimal state of being, you "let go of the stick" and go back to your default settings.

As you continue through this book, it may help to think of your priorities schematic as the schematic of your jet. Keeping an eye on your state is like keeping track of weather conditions; the individual Me factors (as well as your relationship with your partner, kids, family and friends and work) are like the gauges on your jet's dashboard (all of which you'll learn about later in the book).

Some guys even feel that the term "self-care" is too "frou-frou", girly, or "astrologically aligned" for their tastes. If you're one of those guys, think of it as doing your scheduled maintenance or even "pimping out" your private jet so it can be more luxurious and have even better performance.

So make sure your levels are all good and your fuel tank ("ME") is topped up and you'll have the success and happiness that you've always wanted and definitely deserve.

For free tools to help you reset your autopilot and get what the HELL you want go to TheMeFactor.me

The Functioning Workaholic

When the BlackBerry first came out, one of the earlier ads for the new device simply featured a picture of the BlackBerry on a white background with the word "WORKAHOL" underneath it. Workahol for the Workaholic. Like Alcohol for the Alcoholic. That was a badge of honor in the 90s.

I thought this was a brilliant and powerful message. Now, you NEVER had to stop working! It was a smartphone, and although it was aimed at promoting efficiency, what it really introduced to the world was the ability for us to work all the time. We could use our BlackBerries to stay connected (and be on-call to everyone) all the time.

Then along came social media, which, despite appearing to be fun and light, added a whole new level of stress to our lives. Now you get to (have to) keep up with everyone else's life while you try to run your own. It splits your attention several times an hour (sometimes per minute) and forces you to multitask without even knowing it – and multitasking is a productivity killer!

A 2017 article in *Frontiers in Psychology* asks you to test it out for yourself. First, do two tasks separately. Measure the amount of time it takes to complete them. The next time you need to do those two tasks, do them both at the same time. Time yourself again, and then compare the numbers. The results are always the same: when you attempt to multitask, you still get both tasks done, but it takes you longer than it does to do those two things separately. Plus, you're not quite as accurate at the tasks, meaning any time you elect to multitask, you're typically not performing at your best level at any of the things you're doing.

Ultimately, I find that the more things I try to do at the same time, the less efficient I become – and that's not taking into account the part of my brain that's always listening for the "ping" in my pocket.

Something else most people don't realize is that every time you switch focus, there is what is called a "switching cost." According to a study published in the *Journal of Experimental Psychology: Human Perception and Performance (Vol. 27, No. 4)*[1,] switching between tasks requires a significant amount of mental effort. If I'm doing something and my phone goes off, I have to stop what I'm doing and reorient my attention to my phone, which might take some time. Once that's done and I try to get back to my original task, I now have to try to refocus, which, again, takes additional time.

Researchers have measured the time it takes humans to refocus. Regular "brain breaks" have been proven to increase overall productivity, as seen in Francesco Cirillo's time management strategy known as the Pomodoro Technique (many swear by this twenty-five minutes on, five minutes off work strategy). However, frequent interruptions in the middle of task performance, like checking every new email as soon as it pops up, pausing in the middle of a task to respond to a text, or even refilling your cup of coffee, all have negative effects on your overall work output.

Multitasking might make us feel productive, but over the long-term, it only creates more stress: you work harder, but you get less done.

It's especially prudent to reduce multitasking if you're the kind of person who spends half the day scrolling through social media. Every time you log on, it adds to your accumulated stress. You're being flooded in your feed by the extreme highs and lows of the lives of people you know and people you have never met. It's generating a new disorder called "social media anxiety." This is a real thing! Everybody thinks they have to measure up to these unrealistic ideas, achievements, or possessions that people share on their social media channels when, in reality, no one is really living that life.

When you see someone's perfect life on Facebook or Instagram – their dream home or their perfect vacation, doing all the things they love in their spare time and making it look easy – remember to pause for a reality check. Trust me when I say that their lives are not that perfect, and that no one has that all the time.

You're not the only one who's struggling. Everybody feels it. Everybody is thinking, "My life doesn't look that good. I wish my house looked like that. I can't make a cake like that. How come I'm not on vacation like that?" We see the dream vacation. What we don't see is the six years of saving it took to make it happen.

I want to share (with their permission) an experience some of my clients shared with me. They were in Hawaii walking on the beach with their kids. It was a gorgeous day – blue sky, light sea breeze and just the right temperature. From a long way off they saw a woman lying on a log trying to get the perfect selfie with the ocean and beach in the background. She was still working on it as they passed her. They commented about the lengths people go to in order to "prove" how good they have it while missing out on actually having it good! The scary (and sad) thing is that when the family was making their way back more than an hour later *she was still at it*!

It makes *no* sense to compare your life to someone else's (especially when they selectively edit what they chose to show the world).

Superman Syndrome

As men, our lives are unfairly governed by external expectations.

The classic example is when men reach a certain age, and suddenly, everyone is asking them when are they going to get a steady job? They figure that is what they should do, so they go find one. Then people start asking why they have not settled down? "When are you going to get a serious girlfriend?" So they go and get one. Then it becomes, "When are you going to tie the knot?" So they get married. They have barely made it down the aisle before being asked, "When are you going to buy the house?" "When are you going to have a baby?" "When are you going to have a *second* baby?" "When are you going to upgrade to a bigger place?" "When is your next promotion?" It never stops. Trust me.

Men often follow along this progression without giving real thought to whether they have any choice in the matter. They're not invested. They're just doing the "right thing," thinking that it will bring them happiness. And the problem is, even if those things are good, they're not *your* things. They're not your choic-es. If you did not actively and consciously choose them, you're not going to benefit from them or be able to enjoy them. And then, after five, ten, or twenty years, you're tired, pissed off, sick, irritable, and unhappy. And you don't know why.

I see it all the time. Men who have some health problems, or their relationship with their wife has soured. They're drinking too much. They're not sleeping well. And they don't know why.

I'll tell you why. We have never been taught to *think* and make conscious, deliberate decisions to look after ourselves and take responsibility for our own health, well-being, and happiness. Instead, men spend their entire lives running from one crisis to the next, putting out fires and being the hero. Most of us take this so seriously that we lose everything else in our lives – health, relationships, money – and still show up to work and no one ever has a clue that we're just hanging on.

When you live like this, you barely have time to stop and breathe, let alone make a plan or do something healthy for yourself. You think, "As soon as I've fixed this crisis, I'm going to invest some time to do this healthy thing I've always meant to do." But another crisis always comes up. Then another. And another. The goal you wanted keeps getting relegated to the back-burner, and before you know it, crisis management is your way of life. It's a never-ending cycle of sacrificing your own well-being and happiness because of the crisis. Life becomes all about putting out fires.

Don't misunderstand me – there's nothing wrong with making sacrifices. People make *honorable* sacrifices all the time, and that's okay as long as you are clear why you are doing it. If you are choosing to sacrifice something about yourself temporarily as a means to an end and your wife and family are on board with it, it might be a good idea.

Maybe you are working two jobs temporarily to get out of debt or get ahead, or to save for a house or a baby, then that makes sense. But it has to be temporary and it has to be part of a well-thought-out plan. Think about what ten or fifteen years of unhappiness and making poor choices is going to cost you!

Here is a true story. I come from the Caribbean. I was born on an island called Antigua, and my family lived on another nearby island called Montserrat. Montserrat is a small volcanic island that has been actively erupting since the 1990s.

Prior to the 90s, experts thought Montserrat's volcano was dormant and safe. Some cousins of mine, a husband and his wife, moved to London, England to pursue lucrative jobs and were working hard and sacrificing with the goal of saving money so that when they retired, they could move back home to Montserrat. On their little island they were going to build an amazing home looking out on the beach, and everything was going to be wonderful.

To make their dream happen, they made sacrifices. They lived in a tiny apartment in London. They scrimped and saved and set aside their short-term happiness to build their finances. They worked and slaved and offered up their time and energy in the present so they could enjoy their future together. For years they did this, sending money back home to Montserrat to build their dream house.

One day, when they were getting close to retirement, the husband went to see how the house was coming along. While he was away, his wife was walking across a busy street in London and got hit by a bus and killed. That was her retirement. She was done.

The husband came back to London to bury his wife. While he was there, Montserrat did the thing that it wasn't supposed to do: the mountain blew up. The volcano erupted and buried their dream house. They had sacrificed so much, planning for a future they never got to enjoy.

The moral of the story is: if you don't start paying attention *now* to how you use your energy and focus, you'll find yourself working too hard, fighting burnout, going nowhere on a treadmill of notifications, wasting time online, tending to exhaustion, stress, and debilitating anxiety. And for what? A future that could blow up or literally run you over!

Is This Working for Me?

The question you want to ask yourself right now – and often – is this: "Is this working for me?"

Rick Barry is a retired American professional basketball player remembered for shaking things up in the NBA with his unorthodox style. At a time when everybody in the league was shooting free throws overhand, he shot underhand. He didn't care whether the "granny shot" looked cool. It got results! Free throw percentages in the NBA average about 75 percent, but Rick Barry retired with a 90 percent free throw percentage. He did what worked for him.

Compare Rick Barry's story to that of Wilt Chamberlain, a notoriously amazing player with a notoriously terrible free-throw percentage. From 1961 to 1962, Wilt, desperate to improve his free throws, shot underhanded from the foul line. Not only did his free-throw percentage drastically increase, but he sank twenty-eight of thirty-two free throws in his landmark 100-point game—a milestone that nobody in the history of the sport is likely to ever match.

The next season, Wilt Chamberlain did the unthinkable. He reverted to overhand style. Why? Because shooting the granny shot made him feel "like a sissy." The social pressure was too much. Despite the fact that it worked for him, he gave it up.

Ignore what everybody else is doing. You're not asking whether it works for James or Jane. Is it working for *you*?

Depending on your circumstances, your stress level, your tolerance for risk, or any number of other factors, what could work for somebody else might not work for you, and vice versa. It does not matter what everybody else is doing. You have to do what is right for *you*. That is the bottom line. It is also why that focus question, "Does this work for me?" really works.

When my wife and I got married, we chose to have one of us stay at home to raise the kids. That meant we were a single-income family for most of our lives, with less disposable income than other families. We didn't take trips or do things other couples were doing. We also chose to have kids later in life. We are happy with these choices because they worked for us. Even though we were swimming upstream for a lot of it, we were happy. We had a sense of fulfillment and resonance.

What choices do you need to make to create that same sense of fulfillment? They are the key to your happiness.

So, What Is a Psychologist, Anyway? (And Why Should I Care?)

Once you get into the habit of asking the focus question "Is this working for me?" you may get the answer "No" quite often. Then what? Who can help? It's important to know your options so you can stay in control of your own life and make informed choices.

Like many people, you may be wondering what the difference is between a psychologist and a psychiatrist. For that matter, what makes either of those any different from a counselor, a psychotherapist, or a social worker? There are a lot of different specialists doing a lot of stuff that overlaps, and sometimes even physicians don't know the differences between them all.

"Psychologist" is a protected title (as are "registered social worker," "physician," and "psychiatrist"), which means we are licensed by an independent board (such as a college of physicians and surgeons, or a college of psychologists.) We are held accountable by this board. It also means that no one can call himself or herself a psychologist unless they have a certain level of education, have undergone extensive training, have passed tests, and are licensed by the board.

A professional with a protected title can lose their license for behaving inappropriately. They can be sued. Their governing body can sanction them. There is a mechanism in place that, if people are not satisfied with the service they receive, or if the professional acts inappropriately, unprofessionally, unethically, there is some recourse.

On the other hand, the titles of "psychotherapist," "counselor," "mental health professional," "mental health aid," "life coach," and similar titles can be used by anyone. They describe no specific level of training and are not protected titles. This means anyone can take a weekend course on these topics—or just make it up—and if you don't like their services, tough shit. There is nothing you can do.

A psychiatrist is a physician (medical doctor) who has gone through medical school and then specialized in psychiatry. They have an MD. A psychologist, in most jurisdictions, has to have some sort of doctorate (a PhD or a PsyD, which is a professional doctor of psychology, or an EdD, doctor of education). That's at least eight years, and in most cases more like ten years, of college or university education. That can mean the average psychologist at a doctoral level has about a third more education than a family physician.

As a medical doctor, the psychiatrist is trained in the biological basis of mental disorders and in the use of psychoactive medications. They typically prescribe medications that help their patients with issues like bipolar disorder, schizophrenia, or depression. Sometimes a general physician or a family physician will prescribe medication for depression or anxiety, but the psychiatrist is a specialist in that area.

A psychologist – that's me – is the person who typically does what's called the "talking cure." We work with individuals to help them do better in whatever aspect of life they might be struggling with or want to improve. The classic image in most people's minds is the doctor sitting in a chair with a notebook, while the patient sits on a couch and talks about life. I don't use a notebook, and it's usually more of a two-way conversation.

I have worked through "talking cures" with enough men by now to know that the problems I've outlined in this chapter are very real. I've dealt with these issues myself and have been on the receiving end of therapy for about the same amount of time that I've been providing help to others. I might not be able to invite you personally to sit down on the couch for a one-on-one discussion with me, but I'm willing to bet you've experienced some of these problems, too.

Men's lack of personal maintenance and the societal pressures to perform to the point of burnout affect us across the board, and these issues are slowly, quietly killing us.

All Work and No Play

The morning I woke up in Lac La Biche, when I was convinced that I was having a stroke, became a real eye-opener for me. It took burning out for me to realize that I had been raised my whole life to be a workaholic.

In my household, my parents always placed a lot of requirements on me to be responsible. They had me look after things and look after people. I was always given a lot of positive reinforcement for taking care of people and for being considerate and thoughtful of others.

There was a lot of validation for putting other people first. I felt like I needed to work in order to please my parents and be worthy of love. I was steeped in the Protestant ethics of "turn the other cheek" and "give the shirt off your back," and I believed this was how you become a good person and that you'd be blessed with happiness as a result.

Despite these seemingly positive values that were instilled in me, I grew up in a dysfunctional family. I was concerned about my mom. I was concerned about my sister. And after college, I had an economic need to pay off my student loan, but I also had a desire to be a good person and fulfill what I felt was my obligation to my family.

My father died before I could finish my PhD, not that we had a great relationship anyway. I was always looking for guidance and for someone to help me figure out how to "do" life. After grad school, when I was working in northern Alberta, I thought the psychologist I was working for would fill some of that role for me. Meanwhile, he simply saw someone working hard who kept overachieving, so he just kept giving me more work. I grew busier and busier, but I didn't want to disappoint him. I wanted to do a good job, so I just kept on going.

The pressure from my mother and family to look after them also increased. I was the go-to guy in my family; I was the reliable one, the one they could call when something went wrong. I was also the one my mother would call whenever there was something in her house that needed to be fixed or if she needed help with some sort of manual labour or do-it-yourself project.

There was a lot of pull from the extended family as well. I was being stretched too thin, and one of the consequences was an eroding relationship with my wife.

My wife and I had moved together from Chicago, IL to Bonnyville, Alberta, Canada, which, as you can imagine, was a significant culture shock. That alone was a strain on our relationship early on. Add in long work days, me driving all over the countryside and staying some nights in motels while she was stuck alone in Bonnyville, plus having to divide my attention between her, my mother, and extended family...well, it's no wonder our marriage suffered.

When I woke up in the hotel that day and didn't know what the hell was going on, I realized something had to change. I had thought I was doing this work to pay off my student loan debt and get ahead. Now, not only was I physically sick and concerned I had done permanent damage to myself, but my wife and I were fighting all the time. We weren't that deep into the relationship – it had only been a few years – so something had to change. As I tried to figure out what would help me most, the idea for The Me Factor surfaced.

Full disclosure: I'm a work in progress. Even as I write this, I am still learning, and it still does not feel natural for me to take care of myself first. That's exactly why I needed a program to help me do it. I'm not perfect at it, but I know that when I stick to the Me Factor System, my life works better.

The Me Factor System was designed so I could organize myself and make the right decisions to help me look after myself, help me have a better relationship with my wife and kids, and help me improve my productivity and actually feel happy instead of tired and pissed off all the time. It's about creating a healthy me; it's about taking responsibility for one's own needs and realizing sometimes a me-first mentality is necessary.

I know it works – it's been tested in the lab of my life.

The old ways still sneak in sometimes. The sooner you can learn and apply these techniques, the better. In the next chapter, we'll tackle some practical first steps by examining how to "fill your tank" in a healthy way by using step one of The Me Factor System: Me Factor Priority Schematic.

Chapter Two

Me Factor Priority Schematic– Why Men Don't do Self-Care (and Why We Should)

After my wakeup call in Lac La Biche, I took a few days off. I talked to my wife, and we decided I had to change jobs.

That was scary for me. Although the job I was leaving didn't pay all that well hourly, I was working enough hours to make good money. And just choosing to set that initial boundary for the sake of my health was difficult for me. I had grown up in a household where my father was a "dry alcoholic" (he didn't drink, but he had every other trait of an alcoholic in spades: rage, anger, and unpredictability). As a result, I had always been hypersensitive about pissing people off. It took a lot of guts for me to quit the job and look for something else. Yet, when I finally did, I was offered the opportunity to buy my current practice, and that's what I did. By doing so, things got a lot better – and quickly. I started following the rules I had set for myself and living by the system I share in this book, and everything got better.

In general, most men tend to think self-care is something only women do, or that it is self-indulgent in some way. They don't understand that their very lives depend on it. I prefer to call self-care 'personal maintenance'. You need to keep your engine running.

Be a Man

The Protestant work ethic is deeply ingrained in our culture whether you're religious or not, and part of that ethic is the concept of rugged individualism. "Shoulder to the plow", "nose to the grindstone", "keep going", "push through", "head down – ass up", "rub some dirt on it". We place special value on guys who can "man up," "soldier on," and, in general, "be a man."

Most men I encounter believe that, in order to "be a man," they have to be independent. They have to be strong. They have to carry the world on their shoulders because that's what makes them valuable. That's what makes them *men*. Everybody wants to be Rambo, John McClain in *Die Hard* or James Bond —the superhero or the action star who's able to handle everything by himself. They want their wives to call them on the Bat Phone so they can heroically solve all the problems and save the day.

There is not much value placed in our current society on working together and/or looking after yourself. Men think asking for help shows weakness. It's a cliché, sure, but this is why men don't ask for directions. A lot of us don't recognize that we are even allowed to ask for help.

Similarly, most men don't even *know* that they need to take care of themselves. We aren't taught these things! We don't understand that we are allowed to look after ourselves because our culture never taught us to, so we continue to "man up" and "soldier on." We see personal maintenance as weak, or we worry that society will see us as being selfish if we indulge in a little self-maintenance.

The truth is, enlightened men understand that in order to be able to give and provide, and to do the things they need to do for other people, they have to be in the best possible working order. Otherwise, nothing else works.

On the flip side, a lot of men *are* selfish. They go out and do activities for themselves – think of the man who buys the sports car instead of the minivan or goes out drinking until 2:00 a.m. on a Wednesday night, leaving his wife at home with a young baby. It doesn't matter what else or who else gets hurt in the process. They can come across as quite selfish, and though it might give them some satisfaction in the short term, their actions are not helping them in the long term.

One reason for this is that most men don't know what to do for personal maintenance. Most men don't understand that sleep is important, for example, or the importance of getting enough to eat at the right times. They don't understand that talking to somebody to get perspective on their lives and choices would be helpful and shows intelligence. They'll spend time and money getting golf lessons or working out at the gym or going to the dentist, but they won't talk to somebody. They don't see that mental hygiene is as important as dental hygiene.

Knowing where you can get help – through coaching, reading self-help books like this one, or seeing a psychologist like myself – is when you will start to see your life pivot. When I say, "help," I mean gaining an understanding of how you can improve your life as opposed to suffering through it.

In general, men focus more on the cure than on prevention, and rarely if ever do they think about enhancement. The idea is, nothing's broken if I can still limp through it. If I'm not bleeding from my eyes, I should be okay. I'll just keep going. The truth is, we men could be doing things a lot easier and faster – and with a lot less effort – and actually be more successful.

Finally, the main reason that men don't normally do personal maintenance is that there is a stigma around doing some of the work I'm talking about. We live with the implication hanging over our heads that if we can't do things a certain way, we are *weak* – the dirtiest four-letter word in the dictionary. For a man, nothing is worse than being weak.

For some men, even buying a book like this feels like weakness, but it's not. Taking responsibility for your own well-being is the furthest thing from weakness. Being responsible for your own well-being and showing love, generosity, and patience takes strength and courage. It's also the RIGHT thing to do! If you really look at the most successful men you can think of, whether in sports, business, science, or whatever, you find they all have coaches and people who help them – not just within their field or specialty but also with managing their households, their finances, and their lives in a healthy way.

You are the goose that lays the golden eggs. You create your success however you define it, and if you're not in good working order, you can't produce what you need.

What We Can Do About It

It is *responsible* to look after yourself, especially if you have people who are counting on you.

You have to look after yourself in order to look after other people. You're too important not to, and your mission in life is too important for you not to bring your best self to it. Isn't that the version of yourself you would like to share with your friends and family, your clients or colleagues, and the people you care about?

Looking after yourself is an investment. Because when you do, *everything* else goes better. I've worked with clients for a number of years, and many have come back and said, "If I hadn't done this for myself, I wouldn't have gotten X [the contract, a new job, my wife's great opportunity, the chance to travel and so on]."

But we don't invest. We spend all our time and effort on everyone else. Between our work ethic, the idea of rugged individualism, being the action star, neglecting the importance and value of seeking help, and worrying about the stigma of weakness, we are setting ourselves up for major failure.

As an aside, when it comes to my Protestant work ethic, one of the things that really helped me was when I actually *read* the New Testament. It showed that Jesus communed alone and looked after himself first, even before he started his ministry. He went out for forty days alone in the desert. Whether you're a Christian or not, you can understand this. It was "me time!" He was getting his head together before starting his ministry. There is a recurring theme of Jesus taking time to commune with the Father, alone, before he went out and did his thing that day.

The first secret to being a success at personal maintenance is to make it a priority, which is easier said than done. If you are like most men, you have been taught to put everyone/everything else ahead of your own stuff on your list of priorities.

In truth, your #1 priority should be you. That's right. You. I am hereby giving you permission to put *you* back at the center of your own life. Here is what that would look like:

ME FACTOR PRIORITY SCHEMATIC

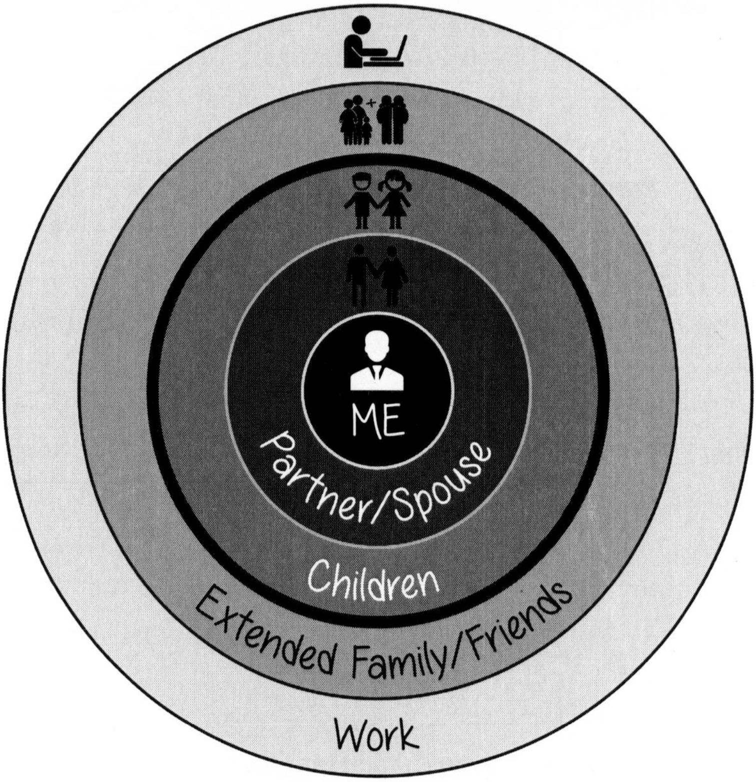

©Copyright 2018 Dr. Ganz Ferrance

Use the tools to help you get what the HELL you want. Download free copies of this and all my graphics at TheMeFactor.me

At the center of The Priority Schematic is the category of "Me". You are #1.

I know what you're thinking. "Putting myself at the *center*? That's so selfish." This is a very common reaction. We tend to think that if you make it a priority to look after yourself, you must be selfish. I used to call this system the "Me First" strategy, but my clients lost their minds at the very idea! Me First? They did not like that title one bit!

The Me Factor Priority Schematic is an inside-out priorities list, and the only way it works is if you have the elements in the correct order:

1. Me
2. Partner/Spouse
3. Children
4. Extended Family/Friends
5. Work

The order of the priorities is the exact opposite in most men's lives. However, this is the correct order for gaining optimal health, abundance, and energy in every aspect of your life.

The order of this list does not vary from person to person. The only thing that varies is where we attempt to pour our energy into the system. The center is the same for everyone whether they know it or not, and the mistake is trying to fill the categories up in the wrong order.

Think of those champagne glass cascades you sometimes see at fancy New Year's Eve parties: a pyramid of stacked glasses with many at the bottom supporting one glass at the very top. The top glass is the "Me" category. Pop the champagne cork, and pour from the top down.

As the top glass gets filled, it overflows and spills over into the next row of glasses. When these are filled, they spill over to the next row and so on until all the glasses are filled. As long as you keep pouring into that top glass, *every* glass gets filled. Try it the opposite way, from the bottom up, and what you'll get is a bunch of empty glasses, one glass that's overflowing onto the floor – and a real mess on your hands.

Guys tend to pour their energy into the "Work" category. As you can see, Work is the outermost circle, the bottom row of glasses. When you pour all your energy there, every other category becomes empty and neglected, and any excess energy is lost. Women tend to pour their energy into either the Children or Partner/Spouse category, which is still not ideal.

Just about every decision we make is based, consciously or otherwise, on which of these categories receives the bulk of our energy reserves. When the system is working perfectly, energy pours into the center (you) and flows outward. Every row is filled to the point of overflowing, and the more you pour in, the better the entire system runs.

Learning and embracing this "Me First" philosophy places you miles ahead of the majority (it's kind of your "unfair" advantage). Time and time again, I have seen that the only way to fill every row with the bubbly is to arrange your priorities in the order listed above. Pour energy into yourself first and work your way outward to the other categories, and you will find your life filled to the point of overflowing – the kind of abundance you never thought you could experience.

Why? Because you can't help anyone else until you first help yourself.

When you are on an airplane and the flight attendants are reviewing the safety precautions before takeoff, they always say, "In case of emergency, put *your own mask on first*."

That sounds terrible, doesn't it? It sounds mean. It sounds selfish! But it is good practice, because if *you're* not safe, you can't help anyone else.

I was once talking about this while I prepared for a speaking event. My daughter was about five years old at the time, and I asked her what she thought. "Why should you put your own mask on first?"

"Duh, Dad," she said. "You gotta put your own mask on first. Otherwise, you have two dead people."

My five-year-old gets it. So how come it took me so long to get it?

You have to put yourself first! Because if you're struggling while trying to help somebody else – anybody else – it's over for both of you. If you want to help and support the person you care about, you can't afford to go down with the ship.

Everything starts from inside and works its way out. Again, you can pour energy into *any* category in the Me Factor Priority Schematic, but the only way you can fill every category is if you pour energy into the center: the Me category. Once the center fills up, it spills over to the successive levels.

Pre-Flight Safety Check?

> *You cannot give from an empty vessel; To give to others, you must fill yourself*
>
> – Chinese Proverb

We tend to pour our energy just about anywhere *but* the "Me" category, and we suffer from that decision every day in the form of burnout and stress overload.

Every day before you "take off", check your fuel level. In fact, it's probably smart to keep your eye on this gauge all day long.

If your "Me" tank is full, everybody in your system benefits from the contribution of your energy. You are fueling your system when your tank is so full it is overflowing with energy.

Let's check your fuel gauge. Use a pen or pencil to indicate the level of fullness of your tank at this particular moment. (You can check this every day, by the way.)

PRE-FLIGHT SAFETY CHECK

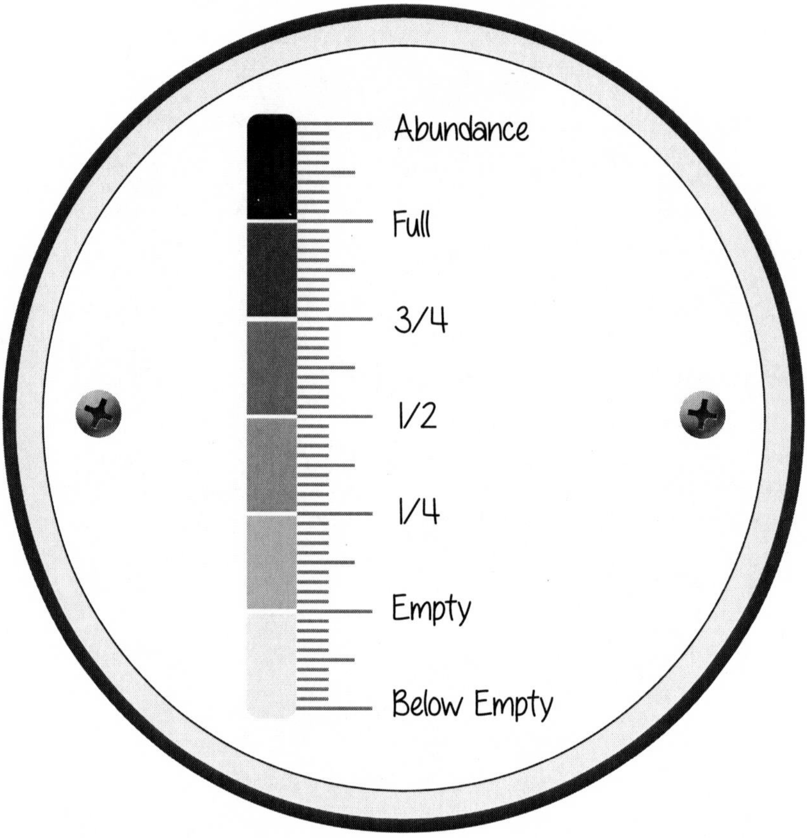

©Copyright 2018 Dr. Ganz Ferrance

Filling Your Tank: What fills your energy tank? What activities give you energy and joy?

Emptying Your Tank: What things or activities currently drain you? What saps your energy?

Use the tools to help you get what the HELL you want. Download free copies of this and all my graphics at TheMeFactor.me

One of the first things they teach you in lifeguard school is how to protect yourself so that *you* don't drown. This involves strategies that can seem almost brutal! For instance, if a swimmer is drowning and trying to pull you down with them because they are panicking, you are taught to knock them out in order to be able to rescue them. Or you wait until they pass out, then pull them out and revive them.

The one thing you do not do is let a drowning person pull you down and wear you out. You are their only hope. You have to be strong in order to help them. This is why one of the most important aspects of the Me Factor System is the concept of *boundaries.*

Setting Boundaries

> *"Good fences make good neighbors."*
>
> Robert Frost

The edges of the five areas of Me Factor Priority Schematic are boundaries, and boundaries are a big part of the Me Factor System. *Nothing* gets past a boundary unless it is beneficial (or, at least not detrimental) to *everything* inside the boundary – all the way down to the "Me" circle.

My idea of boundaries is a double-walled fence with gates. If something is trying to get in – an idea, a concept, an activity, or a person – you open the outer gates and you can analyze the person, place or situation there, in a safe place where it's not going to interfere with anything at your core. (By the way, the boundaries between your children and everything else should be like the Great Wall of China. They're big and thick. They should have barbed wire at the top and an alligator-filled moat. It's important that nothing get through that boundary unless they have been rigorously vetted and are worth letting down the drawbridge for.)

Now, here's the catch: These gates *only* open outward.

If you determine that it's safe to let something in, you can open the inner gate and let it in. If it's not safe, you open the outer gate, push it back out, and lock down the whole system. This is how boundaries work.

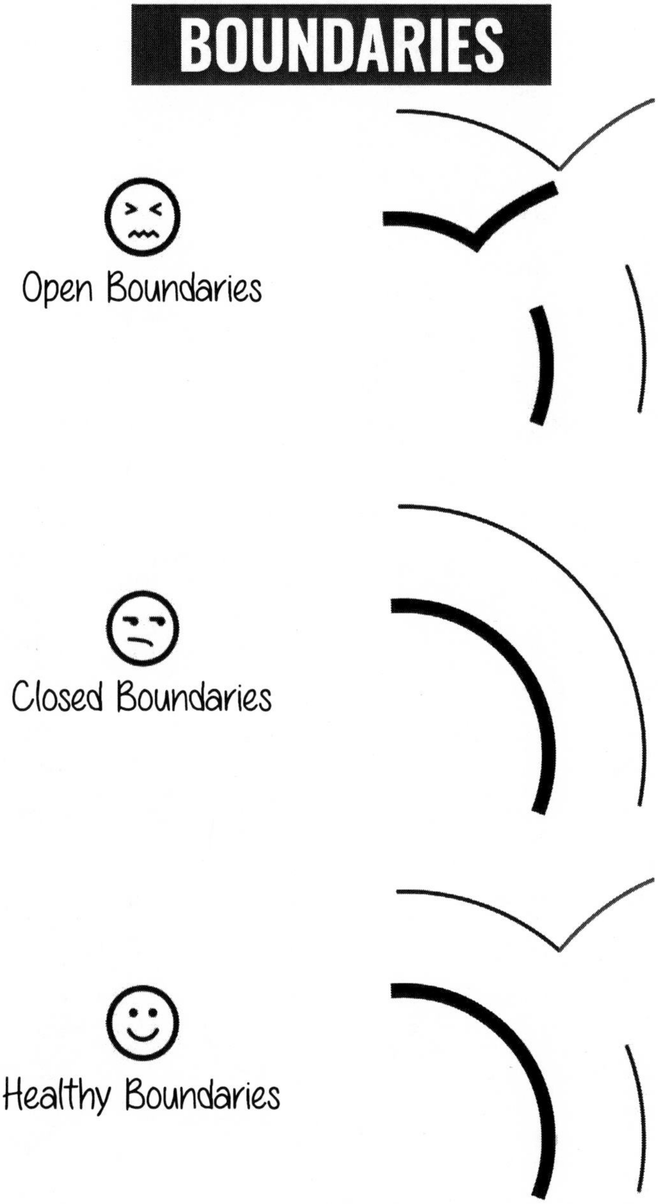

©Copyright 2018 Dr. Ganz Ferrance

Use the tools to help you get what the HELL you want. Download free copies of this and all my graphics at TheMeFactor.me

There are three basic kinds of boundaries:

1. Open boundaries
2. Closed boundaries
3. Healthy boundaries

Open Boundaries

An open boundary is where all sets of gates are open all the time. Anything that gets near your neighborhood can waltz up to your front door and go right into the house if it wants. Needless to say, that's not good. Having no boundaries at all can cause you to become depleted.

You probably know a lot of people like this. They are accommodating, kind, and polite – people-pleasers and helpers. They are often doing everything for everybody else.

I've been like that myself in the past, and I know the effect such thinking has on your decision-making process. Somebody would suggest an idea to me, and I would think, "Well, I'd better go along with it, because I want to please this person." But I was letting anything and everything in that front gate, and I quickly found that by doing this, all my energy was leaking out.

Think of the people who volunteer for everything, or always do whatever others ask of them. This kind of person is usually the one everyone counts on. They're the one everyone calls a "saint," when, really, this person is becoming more and more tired and ultimately ends up sick and wearing themselves out – or jaded, pissed off, bitter, and resentful. Sound familiar?

Closed Boundaries

The closed boundary is the exact opposite; both gates are closed 100% of the time. You're walled off. You don't let in any new ideas, and you don't interact well with people. Unfortunately, some people think that having boundaries at all means they must be closed all the time, and that's not true. Closed boundaries deplete you because you have no interaction with anyone else. You can wither and die – not because other people and priorities are sucking your energy but because there's no enrichment coming in. You deplete yourself because there's nothing new in your life and you do not let anyone contribute to you or your life.

A classic example of a man with closed boundaries is Ebenezer Scrooge from *A Christmas Carol*: an old, crotchety guy living alone in a big house who won't turn on the heat because he wants to save money. He doesn't let anybody in, and he's suspicious of everything and everyone in the world. There's no joy there; it's a dead life.

As you can imagine, people with closed boundaries don't survive very long.

Healthy Boundaries

While you do want to close your metaphorical gates to block out the negative influences, people, habits, and situations, you first have to definitively figure out whether or not something is good. This means you have to be somewhat open to at least checking things out. Then you can decide to close yourself off from something because you know it won't work for you.

That process of careful examination takes courage. It's easier to say, "yes" to everyone and try to be a people-pleaser than it is to tell them "no" sometimes. By the same token, it's easier to be pissed off at the world and scare everybody away with your scowling than to practice discernment. The difficult thing is to be open, hear people out, gather information, and *then* say "no" if you have to, even when somebody makes a good case. That is what maintaining a healthy boundary looks like.

Perpetually Evolving Perfection

Before we move on, I would like to address something about the entire concept of personal maintenance. Men tend to think that if something requires care, it must mean that it's broken. That concept is patently false. We are not out to "fix" anything here. Instead, let me suggest a new mindset: that you are already perfect.

Objective perfection doesn't exist, but we *can* be perfect for who we are and what we know. My daughter was five when she started playing baseball. Not t-ball. *Baseball.* The ball was thrown at her, and she was expected to make contact if she hoped to get on base. Considering she'd never swung a bat before – and that five-year-olds are not necessarily coordinated – the fact that she even hit the ball was pretty good. You wouldn't expect a five-year-old to perform like a major league baseball player. For her level, that was perfect for who she was at the time.

Your personal maintenance journey is not an attempt to "fix" yourself because you're "not good enough." Each of us has our own experiences, our own backstory, and our own level of physical and emotional strength. Wherever we are, whenever we get there, we are perfect.

This is a much more empowering place to start than to think we're broken and have to fix something. I use the acronym PEP, which stands for Perpetually Evolving Perfection. It translates into "I'm already perfect, and I now get to evolve in whatever direction makes sense to me. Wherever I want to go."

In the next chapter, we'll take a more detailed look at the specific dimensions of personal maintenance by examining The Seven Me Factors, a system you can use if you feel yourself starting to slip or feel like your life is not as fulfilling as you would like. You can use this system to determine what's missing and what areas of your life need to be tweaked.

Chapter Three

Develop Your Me Factor Owner's Manual – The Seven Me Factors

To review, the order of the Me Factor Priority Schematic is:

1. Me
2. Partner/Spouse
3. Children
4. Extended Family/Friends
5. Work

Work and Extended Family/Friends can be interchangeable in position to some extent, depending on your situation, but they should always occupy the bottom of your priority list. There is no leeway between the Partner/Spouse category and the Children category: it's very important that your partner or spouse (if you have one) comes in ahead of your children (if you have them).

The big idea is that *you* have to be the #1 priority because you are the capacity. You are the golden goose. You are the machine – the engine driving the ship that carries everything outside of yourself.

Work was where I poured all my energy for a long time, and all it brought was more work. The work never stopped. The more work I did, the more people wanted more work from me. There was no payback in terms of fulfillment, happiness, or peace. If you have your priorities in order, everything flows. You fill up the center, and the rest of the system prospers as a result. On the other hand, if you try to work from the outside in, there is often minimal payoff and damaging side effects.

What does it look like to "fill up the center"? Here is a little experiment for you.

Think about a time when you felt really well rested. You had a really good sleep. You had just come back from vacation, maybe, and you were well fed. You had just eaten a delicious meal, food that was both nutritious and satisfying. You felt good about your life. You were happy. Your Me category was filled with energy. Now, I ask you: If you felt like this on a daily basis, do you think you'd be better or worse as a partner or spouse?

Let's say your partner is also smart and reads this book and does the same thing. He or she is also really happy and healthy and well fed and fulfilled. Do you think they would be easier or harder to get along with?

Let's continue down the line. Do you think if you and your spouse were both fulfilled, you as a couple would be better or worse parents? If your kids learn from you and have a great time with healthy, happy parents, do you think they'd be better or worse as people?

If you get your shit together and have a fulfilled spouse and happy children, your interactions with family and friends are going to benefit exponentially. Don't you think you'd be a better family member or friend if you were happy and fulfilled than if you were depleted, angry, and frustrated?

Then, when Monday morning comes along and work shows up, you can go to work knowing you are fulfilled, your spouse is happy, your children are doing great, and your relationships with your family and friends are in order. Your boundaries are set up. The energy is flowing. And you jump out of bed ready to tackle the day.

Most people think placing Work on the outside of Me Factor Priority Schematic means it won't get the best of you. But if you have the right system in place, you're feeling fulfilled, and work actually gets *more* of you instead of less because you're looking after yourself (assuming, that is, that your job is right for you; but more on that later.)

Do you know the kind of suffering kids go through when their parents are busy and tired and pissed off all the time? You may have known families like this. I hope you're not that friend, the guy who's so tired and pissed off and overworked that he can't keep appointments, can't keep commitments. That's not much of a friendship. Everything suffers when the wrong priority is in the center of your life.

The Dimensions of the "Me" Circle

Pouring energy into the center means you have to make choices based on who you are and what's important to you, as opposed to what's important to everybody else. The problem is, most people don't know how to do that. How do you feed your goose? You do it by addressing The Seven Me Factors.

If you were to dissect the center of your Me Factor Priority Schematic and take a closer look at the category of "Me", here is what it would look like:

THE BALANCE INDICATOR

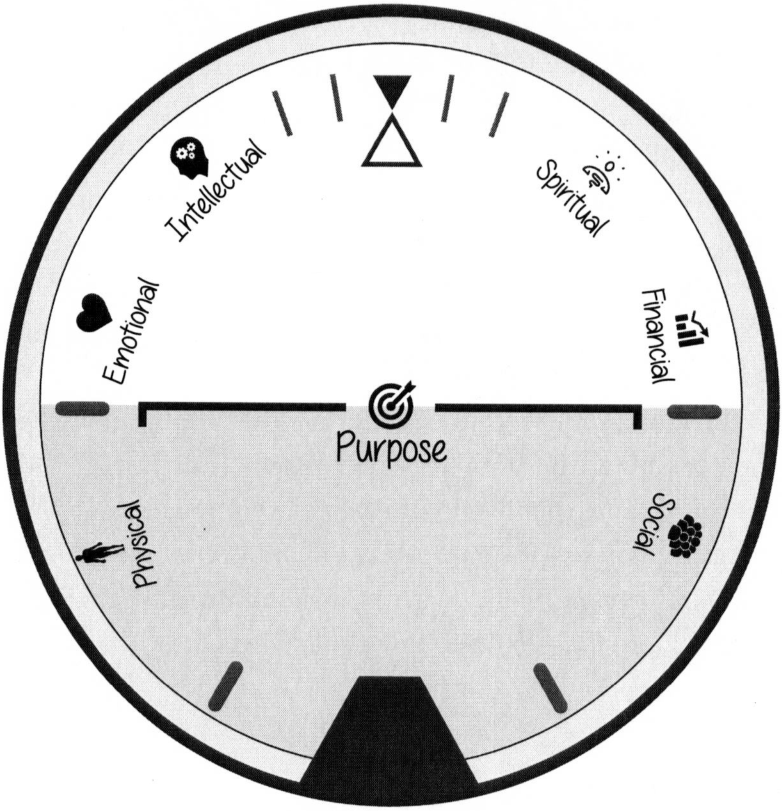

©Copyright 2018 Dr. Ganz Ferrance

Use the tools to help you get what the HELL you want. Download free copies of this and all my graphics at TheMeFactor.me

The Seven Me Factors

We'll look at each of The Seven Me Factors later in this book. For now, here's an overview.

1. Physical

This is your physical plant, like an automobile factory or other manufacturing facility. It influences everything – how you feel, how you function, how you get around in the world. If, say, the air conditioning in your manufacturing facility is not working properly or the machinery needs maintenance and isn't working at maximum capacity, you're not going to get the productivity you need.

Your physical well-being is extremely important to how you feel, how you function, and how productive you can be. Getting enough sleep, proper nutrition and eating at regular intervals, exercise, and taking time off are all part of the physical dimension.

2. Emotional

I know men don't like this category, but it's essential to look after your emotional well-being. That means having healthy emotional outlets. A lot of men hold things in and think it's wrong to show emotion at all. But emotions, even anger, are healthy. They need to be processed, experienced, and expressed in a healthy manner.

Where we get in trouble is when we try to express emotions in unhealthy ways or, at the other extreme, stuff them down, where they in turn leak or explode out when we're not looking. Emotions will come out one way or another, so you might as well be in charge of making sure they come out in a healthy way.

3. Intellectual

Your brain functions like a muscle. If you don't use it, it starts to atrophy. Feed the intellectual part of yourself, as you do the rest of your body. If you don't, your brain starts to literally shrink! Your intellect will diminish. You won't be as sharp.

This becomes a real issue as we age, because if we don't keep our minds active, we are more susceptible to age-related mental decline.

4. Spiritual

What I mean by "spiritual," is being in contact or being aware of something larger than yourself, whether that is an entity or the connection with humans, other life forms, or the subatomic particles in the universe. What it really means is realizing that there's more to life than what's going on in our heads or in front of our eyes presently. It's that sense of appreciation, that sense of awe, joy, and contentment.

Spirituality is very different than being religious. We'll get into this in more detail later. For now, suffice it to say that religion does feed the Spirituality factor. But in many cases, religions – especially organized religions – can also work *against* your spirituality. They can be restrictive, punishing, and lead to a lot of guilt and shame. For me, spirituality is something that is uplifting, kind, and connects people as opposed to dividing them.

5. Financial

The Financial Factor is something we might not really think about as a Dimension of Me, but it takes up a lot of our time and effort.

Money is the number one cause of individual stress and anxiety. In a 2014 study by the American Psychological Association, 72% of survey responders said they had felt stressed about money in the past month. Money is also the number one cause of relationship issues with your partner.[2] Add that to the basic fact that you need money to provide food, shelter, and safety, and this is a factor you cannot afford to overlook.

6. Social

Humans are social beings. That's one of the advantages we have as humans: We divide labor so we don't all have to do everything We share insights so no one of us has to understand everything. I'm good at psychology, you're good at something else, and we can talk to each other and collaborate to build a better world. People play many different roles to keep our society running, but one of the things that helps us be healthy is knowing that we're connected to other people through social interactions.

According to an article in *Psychology Today*, one of the biggest causes of depression and alcoholism is simply being lonely.[3] England just appointed their first "Minister of Loneliness" because the government understands the health, societal and financial costs of loneliness on their citizens[4]. Loneliness also increases production of stress hormones, and individuals who live alone – no matter what their age – are at a higher risk of suicide [5]. We all need solitude to some degree, but when you're by yourself too much, there is something missing. We start to feel discontented, perhaps even unbalanced. This is why social connections are important.

7. Purpose

The last Me Factor is Purpose, and this is a big one. It's foundational. That's why I located it at the center of your balance indicator. When you have a sense of purpose in your life, your life is simply better. Studies show that seniors who believe they have a sense of purpose live seven to eleven years longer than seniors without a sense of purpose.

I often hear cases of people who retire, or businesspeople who sell their businesses, and die quickly afterwards – sometimes within only a year or two. The shock of losing their sense of purpose is too hard on them. Suddenly, there is no reason to get up in the morning. There is nothing that gives them a zest for life. Discovering your sense of purpose comes down to (1) figuring out how to be happy, and (2) learning what you can bring to the world.

Check the gauges on your dashboard.

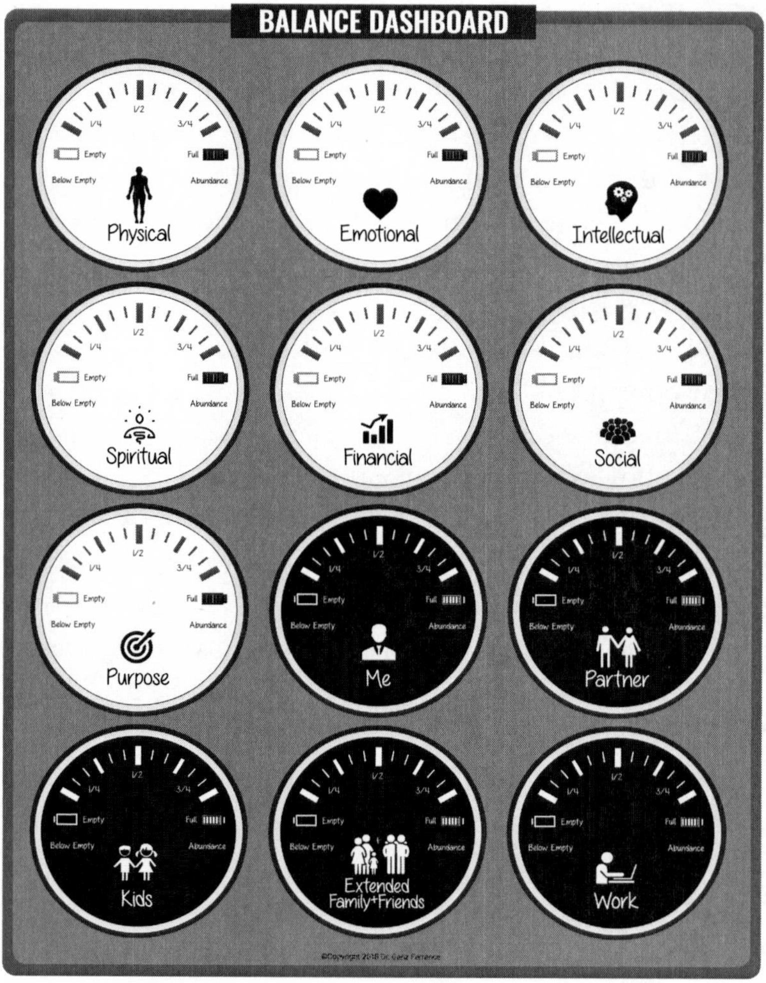

The Me Factor Owner's Manual

Imagine you have everything in order in your life. This is not an unattainable fantasy. If you can keep these seven factors in balance, your life will get better – I guarantee it. But maintaining that balance can be tricky, so I've developed the following worksheet to help you implement your new game plan.

The foundation of the Owner's Manual is activities that you know from experience fulfill you in that specific area of your life. Start filling out your Owner's Manual by brainstorming activities for each of the seven Me Factor categories. As you read the chapters on the individual Me Factors, you'll see suggestions of rejuvenating activities to use to fill out your worksheet in greater detail.

ME FACTOR OWNER'S MANUAL

List as many activites as you can in each area that would fuel that area of your life and help you fill your energy tank.

Dimensions	Activities that Strengthen and Fuel Each Dimension
Physical	
Emotional	
Intellectual	
Spiritual	
Financial	
Social	
Purpose	

©Copyright 2018 Dr. Ganz Ferrance

Use the tools to help you get what the HELL you want. Download free copies of this and all my graphics at TheMeFactor.me

Finding the Balance

In any given period of your life, you may tend to focus more on one Me Factor than another. For instance, you might currently be fairly happy with your physical attributes but you're struggling in the Social category. Or maybe you currently feel strong in the Emotional category, but your finances could use some work.

When I start to feel angrier or more frustrated than usual (Emotional), I can take a look at my Me Factor Owner's Manual and realize, "No wonder! I've been losing sleep!" (Physical) Or, "Man, it's been a while since I journaled." (Spiritual) Or, "You know what? I really haven't read a good book in a while." (Intellectual) Or, "I should call a friend." (Social) This system tweaks your mind so you remember what you need to do to keep improving your life.

This is a dynamic process. In the quest for Perpetually Evolving Perfection (PEP), you're never "done." Your life will shift and the Me Factors are a strategy to help you focus that change where it's most needed to keep you a balanced man.

This system grows with you. The idea is not to beat yourself up if your life is not where you think it's supposed to be, because there is no top. You can keep going and keep getting better at it all the time.

It's okay to be a work in progress. You don't have to be perfect in any one area or even in all seven areas at the same time. You are not broken, but you can always be improving. The question is, how good can you stand to be?

Decision-Making Using the Me Factor System

Uncertainty is a universal source of stress; it's simply part of being human. Making a decision reduces stress but making a bad decision can add exponential stress and anxiety to your life. Fortunately, the Me Factor System helps you make decisions quickly and efficiently, based on what's right for you.

I once was in a workshop with a man (lets call him Richard) who was trying to figure out why he was so exhausted. He was deciding whether to move out of his current apartment he was sharing with someone else. I walked him through the Me Factor Decision Matrix to have him see what it would look like to stay with that roommate, and what would it look like if he moved out.

As we examined all the aspects – including running the financials – he found that by staying with his roommate he was perpetuating the exhaustion. He suddenly realized why he was so tired all the time.

Although he ended up choosing to stay, he now understood what was causing the exhaustion, knew there wasn't anything wrong with him and made his choice to stay based on facts. It wasn't financially feasible for him to move out yet, so he made sure he built in activities and personal maintenance techniques that would recharge him. He looked at all The Me Factors and started giving himself more of the positive things that filled his

"Me" circle. This balanced out the energy drain caused by his living situation.

Another man in one of my workshops, (let's call him Charles), had been struggling with his job. He hated it but was scared to leave and didn't know what to do. We did the same exercise; he had planned to go to a job interview that afternoon, so we ran this through the Me Factor Decision Matrix. We quantified the situation and determined that the job he was interviewing for was far more favorable than the job he had been working at for twelve years. He was so excited that he ran out and went to the interview. He later emailed me to tell me he had taken the job that very afternoon. He said, "Thank you so much for that. It helped me clarify what matters right away."

For step-by-step walk-throughs of this decision-making process, and the results for Richard and Charles, check out the Decision Matrix in Chapter Eleven.

Unresolved decisions drain energy, even small ones. Managing little decisions by addressing them the right way – consciously and deliberately, taking into account all the things that are important to you – is essential. It means seeing the whole picture, so you're not forced to compromise one factor to serve another. You are making sure it all fits. And if you do have to lose a bit in one factor, you understand that *before* you make the decision, so you can factor that in and see if that decision is still worth it.

In most cases, we are swept along by consensus, adhering to what everybody else wants or doing what everybody else does.

Learning how to make decisions that are right for you, as opposed to going with the flow or making decisions without giving them sufficient thought, is an important key to happiness, well-being, and peace of mind.

In the following chapters, we will break down The Seven Me Factors one by one and examine how to use them to make conscious, informed decisions based on what's best for you.

Chapter Four

Physical, Part 1: The Performance Arousal Curve

The quest for high productivity is a huge drive in our society—to get more done and collect more of those precious golden eggs. Our culture teaches us to push harder.

Well, I have news for you! The landmark research by Yerkes and Dodson says that this is not the whole story. Pushing harder often works to your detriment, as the Yekes-Dodson Law and the Performance-Arousal Graph show.

The Performance Arousal Curve

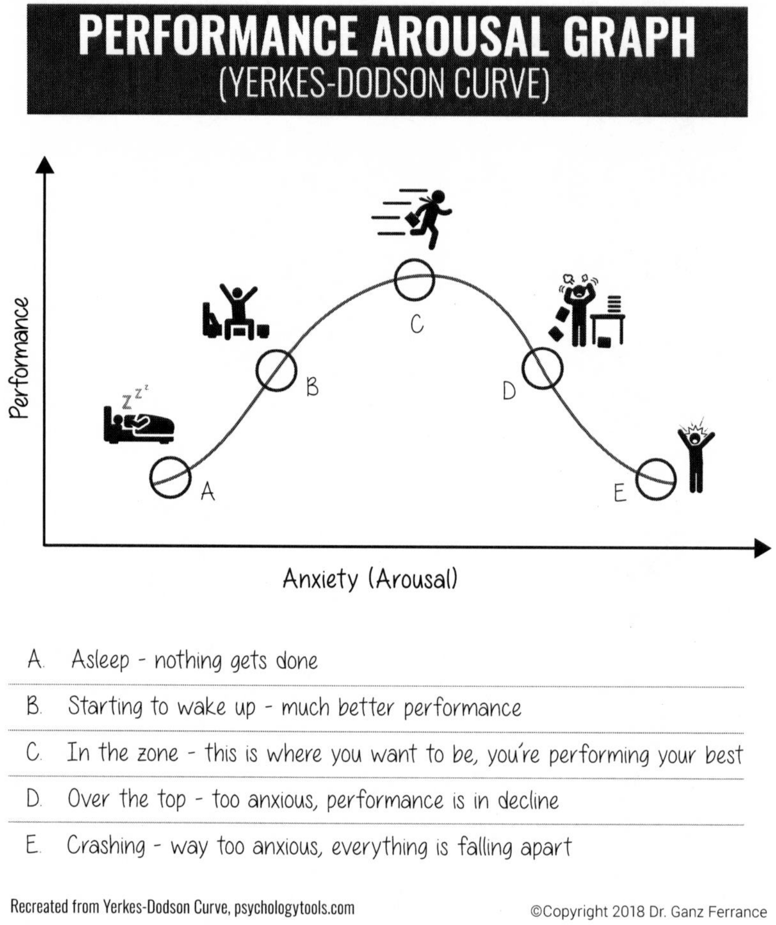
PERFORMANCE AROUSAL GRAPH
(YERKES-DODSON CURVE)
Performance
zzz
A
B
C
D
E
Anxiety (Arousal)
A. Asleep - nothing gets done
B. Starting to wake up - much better performance
C. In the zone - this is where you want to be, you're performing your best
D. Over the top - too anxious, performance is in decline
E. Crashing - way too anxious, everything is falling apart
Recreated from Yerkes-Dodson Curve, psychologytools.com
©Copyright 2018 Dr. Ganz Ferrance

Use the tools to help you get what the HELL you want. Download free copies of this and all my graphics at TheMeFactor.me

On the x-axis of the Performance Curve is Arousal (or Anxiety). On the y-axis is Performance. Think of Arousal/Anxiety as effort, physiological stimulation, just staying awake – or sometimes sexual arousal. This curve applies to just about everything you do.

Typically, we are taught (or believe) that the higher the exertion the better the results. In most people's minds, there's a nice dotted line climbing steadily from the bottom-left corner all the way up to the top-right. We think that the more we try, the more we do, the more effort we employ, the better our performance will be. This is simply not true.

Well, it's sort of true for a little while. As you can see on the graph, your performance skyrockets at first. But then you hit a sweet spot. Your output peaks. After that, the process works in reverse. You experience a sharp decline in performance. The harder you try, the worse you do.

For example, let's say you've got your keys and you're walking up to your house after a day at work. You pull out your keys, put them in the lock, open the door, and walk in. People do this millions of times daily all around the world. It comes to us automatically. Really easy, no stress. But what if one day you're walking up to your house, and just as you're about to pull your keys out, a mad dog comes out of the bushes and charges at you. You need to get in the house to protect yourself.

Now what happens? You're running toward the door. You might drop your keys. You pick them up, but you fumble. You try to get the key in. It's the wrong key. You find the right key, put it in the lock, and break the key off. If you're *more* motivated to get into your house, why is your performance *worse*?

The problem is that as you become more aroused, your body enters a state of "fight or flight." Your brain starts to decompensate when it comes to judgment and fine motor coordination. You'd be way better at fighting or running away in this state, but your lock-opening skills definitley go to hell.

The Consequences of a High-Anxiety, Low-Performance Lifestyle

In our Western culture, we tend to believe that as long as we're working, we're steadily climbing uphill. We think we're riding this imaginary incline to the top, fueled by our increased efforts. We think if we try harder, we're going to accomplish more – we'll hit peak performance and just keep climbing forever.

This is a destructive misconception, and the consequences affect your physical, mental, sexual, and physiological performance. If your physiology is too aroused most of the time, your physiological performance is not good. This is what happens if you're constantly under stress or working too hard.

Most men live their whole lives on the downhill side of that graph. We live over the hump, in a state of constant stress, our performance getting increasingly worse.

Living in a state of constant arousal leads to chronic issues: high blood pressure; hardening of the arteries; heart disease; higher risk of stroke, diabetes and cancer; even erectile dysfunction – if you're trying too had to 'get hard', it just doesn't happen. All of these physiological things start happening on top of shitty relationships, a bad time with your kids, poor performance at work, and the subjective experience of feeling stressed.

This is why personal maintenance is not just a "nice idea." It's practical and responsible. It becomes necessary to do anything you can to decrease your state of constant hyper-arousal. This will help you perform better and reduce your exposure to those unhealthy consequences.

Simply put, what we need to do is learn to relax. Slow down. Learn to take life a little easier. As we do so, we become calmer, our anxiety dials back, and our performance increases. Everything just flows.

The Law of Diminishing Returns

LAW OF DIMINISHING RETURNS GRAPH

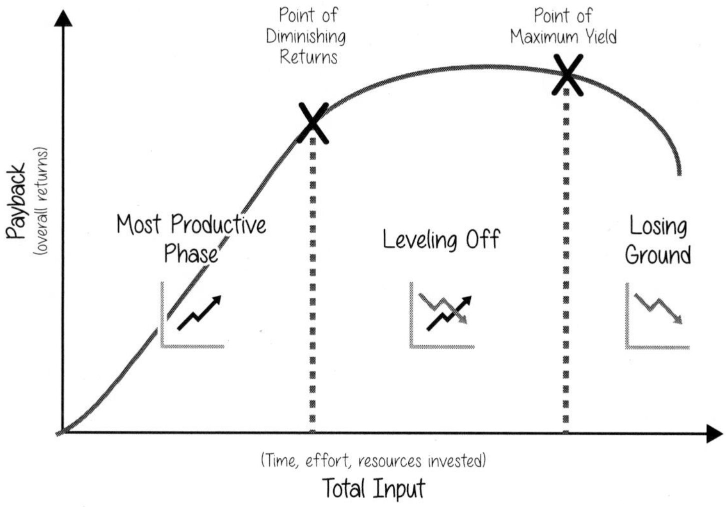

Most Productive Phase
This is where you are your most productive. It pays to invest more time and effort now.

Leveling Off
As more time and effort is invested, your productivity decreases. It is best to stop during this time.

Losing Ground
Consider this the red zone. At this point you have zero or less return on your effort.

Recreated from personalexcellence.co

©Copyright 2018 Dr. Ganz Ferrance

Use the tools to help you get what the HELL you want. Download free copies of this and all my graphics at TheMeFactor.me

The graph above represents The Law of Diminishing Returns and another huge misconception in Western culture. The Law of Diminishing Returns states that adding more of one factor (in this case, time) will at some point yield lower returns. In other words, you will become less efficient over time until you reach a point where you are losing your desired result.

I like to use the example of two guys chopping wood. One looks like the classic lumberjack, a big, burly guy. The other guy looks like Woody Allen, a skinny, weak-looking accountant type. Both are chopping wood. The lumberjack goes out at about 8:00 a.m. and starts chopping. He's at it all day. He stops once for a quick fifteen-minute lunch, eats, and then gets back to it. By 5:00 p.m., he's sweaty and exhausted from working hard all day—and he has a nice pile of wood.

The skinny guy gets up at the same time, starts working at the same time, and chops wood for about fifteen minutes. At 8:15 a.m., he stops, takes a sip of water, pulls out a file, sharpens his axe, then chops wood for another fifteen minutes. Our Woody Allen character does that all day. Every fifteen minutes, he's stopping for a break and sharpening his axe. He stops for lunch, too, but instead of fifteen minutes, he takes an hour. He takes a little nap, sharpens his axe again, and goes back at it.

At the end of the day, the skinny guy has got a stack of wood twice as high as the burly lumberjack, plus he's still got energy to go home with. He was chopping wood with a sharp axe. The lumberjack had a dull axe after probably the first fifteen minutes. That's the difference. This story also demonstrates other principles, but my point is that working harder doesn't always mean you're working smarter. Stopping to take a break reduces your rate of arousal. And this doesn't just apply to hard labor. Reducing anxiety allows you to better focus on your work. By taking regular breaks throughout the day, you're sharpening your axe. You're reducing arousal and resetting yourself back to the productivity range of The Performance Curve.

Now, imagine this on a larger scale: taking regular breaks from the daily grind to go to dinner with your partner, take a nap, go for a bike ride, work out, go to the doctor, go on vacation. We tend to tell ourselves that we don't have time; we have too much wood to chop! But the truth is, these activities are about sharpening the tools. And when you're chopping with a sharp axe, your performance increases, and you become more efficient.

How to Avoid Diminishing Returns

It seems logical that we should do everything we can to avoid living on the downhill side of the Performance Curve and to cut down on the effects of The Law of Diminishing Returns. What can you do for yourself physically to improve your performance? There are all sorts of things you can do for yourself to maintain your physical power plant. Here are a few examples of what might work for you.

- Eat nutritious, nourishing foods every three hours, (stopping a few hours before bedtime)
- Drink lots of water
- Exercise
- Get eight hours or more of sleep at night (regularly!)
- Develop a daily routine

Physical is first in the Me Factors because the state of your physical body determines your baseline in all the other categories. If you don't maintain your physical plant, the emotional plant is not going to work, you won't feel in tune with your spiritual side, your relationships won't function well, and so on.

Keep in mind that these are not just thoughtful suggestions; this is like the maintenance schedule for your car. It's your body's essential maintenance program. You know you have to change your oil, rotate the tires, and drain the brake fluid, and it's the same with your body. Drink enough water, eat the right foods, and get adequate sleep. Write this down in your Me Factor Owner's Manual. If you feel burned out, take a look at this list, and you will quickly see what's missing for you and what needs to be added.

Eat Right, and Eat Regularly

When you smooth out the input of calories and nutrition into your body, you also smooth out your glycemic index; you normalize the glycogen response in your body so you don't have energy peaks and valleys. Rather, you have a smooth curve throughout the day. This helps your hormones stabilize, as well as your mood. It helps you feel calm, and it helps you live in that sweet spot on The Performance Curve. Again, this is not just your work performance but how you relate to people, and, more importantly, your physiological performance. Your body is happier, and your immune system is stronger.

Men go about eating all wrong. A lot of guys tend to eat breakfast and then not eat again until supper. Then they'll have a huge supper and figure that's good enough. Or they might skip breakfast entirely, eat one meal a day, and live off coffee and protein bars. I cannot overstate how much stress this puts on your body. It puts your body into a state of fight-or-flight. You're operating in survival mode all day, every day.

I suggest that people eat every two-and-a-half to three-and-a-half hours. This stabilizes blood sugar levels, which stabilizes your hormones, which helps your body to feel soothed. This reduces the "stress alarm" that's constantly ringing in a lot of people's bodies. When you're eating regularly, your body feels like it's being looked after. It knows it has enough calories, which actually soothes the central nervous system.

Exercise

You don't need me to tell you that exercise is foundational to your overall health and an effective way to manage stress. I'm sometimes asked what the best exercise is for reducing stress and making you healthy. The answer is *any exercise at all.*

When you don't know what to do, do any damn thing. Something is always better than nothing. You don't have to run a marathon or do an Ironman triathlon; you just have to get moving.

The January 2008 issue of the *Mayo Clinic Health Letter* stated that exercising for just half an hour a day can lower high blood pressure, help manage your weight, increase your energy, and improve your overall mental well-being. It doesn't even have to be all in one sitting. It can be ten minutes at a time here and there.

If you can do ten minutes three times a day, five times a week that is sufficient to maintain your health. If you want to build your health, as opposed to just maintaining it, you need to do about one hour of exercise three times a week or more. But still, it's not that big of a time commitment. Why do we make this so hard?

We know that one of the main advantages of exercise is its mental health benefits. Once you make exercise a habit, you have a consistent outlet for your stress. In order to manage stress as intended, physical systems in your body have to work together efficiently. When you exercise, those systems get a chance to practice working together. Your heart has to work harder, your brain has to work to coordinate the movements, and your muscles have to work to execute those movements.

Essentially, getting regular exercise is like your body practicing its stress responses. When dealing with stress in everyday life, a body already used to that stress can manage it appropriately.

There has been a great deal of research on the effects of both aerobic and weight-bearing exercise for overall general health. Both force blood to your brain. This helps you focus more easily, improves your memory, and increases your creativity. And one of the first noticeable effects of exercise on your body is its ability to improve your mood. It gives you a lift and helps your brain chemistry to be more positive by releasing endorphins and other "feel-good" chemicals.

Personally, I like mixing up workouts between cardio and weights. With some high intensity cardio mixed with weight-bearing workouts, I feel stronger physically. When I feel physically stronger, that supports emotional and mental well-being. It gives me a boost of confidence, more energy, more capacity to manage stress, and self-assurance to go after my goals. Plus, the knowledge that you're burning fat and toning muscles does wonders for your self-esteem.

Benefits of Exercise

Most of us know we should exercise, but we can't seem to find the time or we just don't enjoy it. Beyond general physical fitness, here are a few extra benefits of regular exercise.

Exercising makes it difficult to concentrate on anything other than the workout. This sort of focus can be like meditation in motion. Many find it extremely grounding to meditate while in motion, especially with rhythmic movements such as rowing, running, or cycling. It gives you a sense of *flow*. Engaging those peak experiences on a regular basis is incredibly healthy for your brain chemistry.

There was an interesting study in the book *Flow,* by psychologist Mihaly Csikszentmihalyi, about the optimal state of consciousness to achieve creativity, positivity, and abundance. This study asked people to list the mindless, everyday tasks they regularly engaged in, like washing dishes, or things they did just for a sense of play, or to lose themselves in the moment. Then they denied these people the ability to do these things for three days.

The researchers found they had to shut the experiment down on ethical grounds after just one day because people were starting to get anxious and stressed. They began exhibiting neurotic symptoms because they weren't able to do these things.

It says a lot about the importance of such tasks that, when a sense of flow was removed from people's lives, strong symptoms of generalized anxiety disorder appeared within a day.

Exercise is one of those things that provide you that sense of flow, so imagine if you had that three times a week, or five times a week, or every day. It is essential to your self-management, your stress management, your sense of joy, and your physical sense of well-being.

CONTROL

One of the things that exercise gives you, especially if you do it on a regular basis, is a sense of control. When we feel out of control – whether because there is ambiguity or uncertainty in our lives, we don't have control of our time, or there are too many open loops – it causes stress.

Exercising is one of the best ways to feel in control. Getting to the gym three times a week, going for a walk, getting out to play your sport, or whatever it might be for you helps you regain control, which can offer stability and autonomy and make you feel like you're in charge of your life.

When you have something in your schedule that you can look forward to, whether it's a sport, a group fitness class, or lifting weights, that sense of anticipation is extremely important for stress management, for being your best self and optimizing your well-being.

IMPROVED REST

Most people who exercise regularly note that they sleep better when they stick to a workout routine. When you have exercised, your body will naturally go into repair mode, and you will experience a much deeper rest.

Since sleep is one of the pillars of good health, your physiology reaps the benefits. You can also manage stress better and will wake up with more energy due to higher-quality sleep.

HEALTHY HUMAN INTERACTION

Everyone needs human contact (see Chapter Eight), and I recommend meeting that requirement by doing a shared activity. Not only can it be very fulfilling, but it also can help to motivate you. Accountability partners can ensure that you stay on track to make sure you show up to the gym. You don't want to let your team down if you're playing sports, and that does really help you be much more consistent with it.

NORMALIZED FIGHT-OR-FLIGHT RESPONSE

Imagine you're walking through the woods, and suddenly a bear rears up out of nowhere. You have three choices. You can play dead (the freeze response), run away (the flight response), or start throwing haymakers (the fight response). Granted, we aren't faced with these scenarios very often in our modern culture. I can't remember the last time a bear tried to eat me, but it's ingrained in us to have the same response to the stress of modern-day life.

Today, the bear has been replaced by traffic jams, rising interest rates, or angry bosses. These are a far cry from a 700-pound grizzly, but *your body doesn't know the difference.* Your body still has the same response to sources of stress, even though the stress you are experiencing no longer has anything to do with survival. We can't really play dead in traffic, we can't run from interest rates, and most of us don't normally beat up our bosses, so we have to do something else with that energy.

Exercise helps us burn off some of that fight-or-flight energy, especially if you are consciously aware that you are burning it off. Hitting the heavy bag, lifting some heavy weights, going for a long run, or playing a game helps you empty that pent-up energy and settle your fight-or-flight response.

FOCUS

Because you increase your heart rate when you exercise, your blood flows through your body a lot faster. It cleans out our systems better and also forces more circulation to your brain, so your brain works more efficiently. A 2017 research review in the British Journal of Sports Medicine[6] found a link between exercise and cognitive function on people over fifty years of age, and the meta-analysis showed that exercise leads to measurable benefits to both the body and the brain.

Any time you fall into a spiral of negative thoughts, the brain wants to reinforce them. The more negative thoughts you experience, the crappier you feel. Your body feels bad. As a result, you start to worry about how bad your body feels, which reminds you of your negative thoughts...and you get into this odd, vicious cycle. When you exercise, you can't do that.

When you work out, you're not stressing. You're not depressed or anxious or worried. You are focusing on the task at hand, on getting through that final pull-up on your next breath, or putting up the next rep, or powering through the next bicep curl. It breaks that cycle because you have to be physically, emotionally, and mentally present. Once that cycle is broken, it's much harder for that cycle to get reestablished in the future.

If you're exercising on a regular basis, you're giving yourself a huge advantage by breaking free of the negativity and relieving any sense of guilt, stress, anxiety, anger or depression.

Exercising Effectively

START SLOWLY

If you haven't worked out in a while, start by walking for ten minutes or simply taking the stairs instead of the elevator. Progression is the name of the game so start with two push-ups and see if you could add one every day until you get to twenty or thirty. A slow, steady start increases your rate of success, and you can build on things from there.

BUILD A HABIT AS OPPOSED TO SETTING A GOAL

Most people approach physical fitness by setting some major goal. There is nothing wrong with setting goals, but if you approach physical fitness as a way of building it into your lifestyle, it's much easier to be gentle with yourself.

So be gentle with yourself. Even if you have a bad day – maybe you were only able to work out for half an hour instead of an hour – celebrate what you have done rather than focusing on what you haven't done. It's okay, because you're trying to establish this as a part of your healthy lifestyle. This is more effective than attempting to meet your goals and beating yourself up when you fall short. Celebrate your victories rather than seeing what you don't accomplish as failures.

If you are going to set goals, set realistic ones. I like micro-goals such as, "I'm going to do two more reps," or, "I'm going to do one more minute," or, "This week, I'd like to do at least three workouts." Micro-goals allow you a sense of celebration and completion fairly quickly and often, which will motivate you and help you stick with it.

I was an emcee for an event where author Michael Beckwith spoke, and I learned the following principle from him: Something is better than nothing, and anything is better than nothing, so be gentle with yourself.

If you did one push-up, at least you started. You did something. It might not be much, but you did something that day, so be generous with yourself.

DO WHAT YOU ENJOY

You don't have to go to the gym and put on spandex if that's not your thing. You don't have to swim or be a gym rat if you prefer the outdoors. If you enjoy walking, go for a walk. Do things you enjoy. You will get the physical benefit as well as the emotional benefit and experience a sense of fun.

TRACK YOUR PROGRESS

First, schedule your exercise. Second, write it down or find a way to track your progress. All the smartphones have tracking apps now. You can use a Fitbit or Apple Watch, or you could go old-school and use a piece of paper. However you measure the stats, you can either then enhance or slow down. If you track what you do, you can actually see trends. That can help you be more successful and more consistent with your exercise.

Mix it up if you can to help you keep your interest, and it is actually more efficient in terms of building your fitness when you vary your workouts on a regular basis. I like P90X because they tend to have a lot of different exercises that you go through within a week. Then you repeat and switch them up every three weeks or so.

GET A TRAINER

If you can swing it, get a trainer. You may find it incredibly helpful – at least in the beginning – to have somebody who can teach you how to exercise properly so you don't hurt yourself. A trainer can teach you some of the fundamentals so you understand what you're doing and why, making it much easier to keep going, understand the benefits, and do it right.

You're Never Too Busy

One of the biggest benefits of exercise is that it really does make you more productive. You are able to focus better, and you're even able to be more creative. I was listening to the Mayor of Edmonton, Don Iveson, on the radio and the interviewer was asking him what his week looked like. He talked about how busy he was, and they asked him how he managed it all.

He said, "Exercise."

He said he was so busy, and he had tried to cut things out so he could spend more time with his family. One of the first things to go was exercise, but then he realized, to his surprise, that it was making him *less* efficient. He had less time, so he put exercise back in and found he was able to do more with less time and ultimately get more time back for spending with his family. One hour of investment gets him three or four hours back in terms of more efficient productivity.

Keep in mind that any time you can do one task or activity that hits multiple "Me" factors, you should take advantage of this. Yoga, for example, can hit the Physical, Spiritual, and Emotional Factors all at once. It can even hit your Social Factor if you're taking a class or attending with a friend or family member. It's always a good idea to choose an activity that offers the biggest payoff.

Chapter Five

Physical, Part 2: Why Men Need Rest

The Physical Factor is so outrageously important to personal maintenance that it simply cannot all be crammed into a single chapter. The previous chapter dealt mostly with the work of maintaining your body. This chapter deals with something that is just as important to your overall health: rest!

As we've seen, neglecting to take regular breaks places you on the downside of The Performance Curve, and the harder we work without rest, the more we are affected by The Law of Diminishing Returns. In fact, rest – specifically sleep – is so integral to your personal physical maintenance that I would argue it is foundational to the entire Me Factor System.

Sleep is prime axe-sharpening time. If you don't get quality sleep, nothing else works. According to research by the National Sleep Foundation, adults ages 18 to 64 years old need between seven and nine hours of sleep per night, and it is not recommended that adults get less than six hours of sleep per night.[7]

As men, we frequently push aside the need for rest. We'll sleep when we're dead, right? Well, if you're consistently getting less than six hours of sleep per night that may come sooner rather than later.

People understand the dangers of driving under the influence. It's safe to say that, generally, we know it's negligent to drive while you're impaired. But "impairment" isn't limited to the effects of substance abuse. The American Automobile Association conducted a study on sleep and its relationship to accidents and found that if you miss one hour of sleep in one night, your chances of getting into an accident almost double.[8] Just one hour of sleep, one night! If you get less than five hours of sleep in a night, your chance of being involved in an accident increases by ten.

I ask you, in light of those stats, how can we *not* consider a lack of sleep as functioning while impaired? If you have a ten times greater chance of getting in an accident when tired than you do if you get your full night's sleep, what does that say about your overall performance across the board?

Sleep and Body Chemistry

Sleep, exercise, diet, and mindset all are important to your physical well-being, but there's only one you can't live without: sleep. Sacrifice sleep, and none of the other stuff works. In fact, cut out sleep entirely, and you die.

Lack of sleep alters your body chemistry. Your body goes into fight-or-flight mode, and any unnecessary processes come to a screeching halt. Your body isn't worried about burning fat or building muscle – you could exercise all day long, but if you don't sleep, it won't do you any good. You could abide by the perfect diet, but without sleep, it's pretty much impossible to lose weight even in ideal circumstances. Your body is too busy just trying to survive.

You may have heard of a circadian rhythm: a biological pattern our bodies fall into with respect to when we sleep, when we wake, and our best time to be functional at certain things. At its core, it is a routine. A schedule. And the more consistent that schedule is, the more effectively your body and mind are able to do what they need to. The better your mind and body function, the better you feel.

Timing is critical. When you stick to a schedule and go to bed at roughly the same time every night, your body gets used to that and starts to prepare itself for sleep ahead of time. It becomes easier for you to fall asleep. You also get higher-quality sleep. Now, obviously, we can't always be exact with our timing, but there is some leeway. The rule of thumb is if you can stay within two hours of your normal bedtime, you typically don't reset your internal clock; your circadian rhythm is only interfered with minimally, if at all.

If you go beyond two hours, that's when it becomes problematic. Typically, what people do – and men are always guilty of this – is: on Friday night, we say, "All right! Weekend's here!" We stay up late, hang out with our friends, go out drinking, and crawl into bed in the wee hours of the morning. Normal bedtime might be ten or eleven o'clock, but on Friday night, we're up until two or three. We sleep in the next day, and maybe do it again on Saturday night. Come Sunday night, we try to go to bed early or at least at a reasonable time to recover because we have to go to work on Monday.

And what happens? We're dragging our ass on Monday. We're miserable. We're somewhat better on Tuesday. By Wednesday, we might feel okay. On Thursday, it's, "I feel pretty good. Can't wait to party tomorrow night!" Friday rolls around, and we start the whole process over again.

I'm not saying you shouldn't party with your friends or that you're not allowed to go out. Just keep it within a reasonable time limit. And if you do deviate from your circadian rhythm, try to get back into it as quickly as possible. If you go out on Friday night, sleep in a *little* bit on Saturday but not too long – this disrupts your routine. Try to get to bed as close to your regular time as possible on Saturday night.

If unforeseen circumstances or something beyond your control causes you to deviate from your routine, products like melatonin can help you get back into your sleep schedule rather than having to tough it out if you're struggling.

Chronic Sleep Deprivation Equals Chronic Impairment

Here's what we know about being impaired: The more impaired you are, the less aware you are of your impairment. You simply don't know how much it's affecting you.

Operating without sufficient sleep is clearly a bad idea. But if missing one hour of sleep just *one time* has such a huge impact, think about the cumulative effect of missing one or two hours a night for a week straight or a month or a decade! What is that doing to your performance?

Sleep is extremely undervalued in our culture. In Arianna Huffington's book *The Sleep Revolution*, she covers the subject in depth and demonstrates how getting a good night's sleep in her own life helped her be more successful.

The best thing about humans is also our biggest problem: We adapt quickly.

A one-time experience of missing an hour of sleep one night can very quickly become the new normal. We quickly adapt and habituate to our less-than-perfect schedule. When people say, "Oh, I can function on five hours of sleep," or, "I only need two hours of sleep and I'm fine," the truth is that they've gotten used to under-performing. They've gotten used to being tired – basically, they've adapted to being chronically impaired.

Research shows that shift workers typically live about seven years less than the average worker.[9] Part of that reason is that they're simply losing sleep, but a lot of it has to do with the fact that their circadian rhythm is constantly being interfered with.

Men Need Sleep

Sleep is the foundation of all beneficial biological processes. It's the only time your body heals, the only time you replenish your brain chemistry, the main time you build muscle.[10] So, when people don't sleep, they're not their best – especially men.

As guys, we think it's manlier to not sleep or to just be tough. It's not uncommon to hear men say things like, "Sleep is for the weak." But, as we've seen, when you don't sleep, you are not at your best. Your brain is foggy, you're more irritable, you're not as creative, and your ability to handle stress and solve problems deteriorates. You get yourself into far more trouble and are far less efficient when you don't have proper rest.

How to Get More Sleep

The old wives' tale is that every hour of sleep before midnight is worth two after midnight. It may not be quite that simple, but the quality of sleep – and the benefits you receive from sleep – are greater toward the *end* of your sleep cycle than at the beginning. Your body needs a certain amount of uninterrupted sleep to reach that valuable, restorative REM stage of sleep. You need high-quality, uninterrupted sleep, a consistent bedtime, and a consistent wake-up time.

One of the things that helps you get a good night's sleep is to end your screen time about an hour before you go to bed. A half an hour will work as well, but an hour is ideal.

A lot of people end the day by watching TV, checking social media, or reading on their devices in their bedrooms. When they do that, two things happen: first, the strobe effect of the changing images on the screen changes your brain chemistry and reduces the production of melatonin, meaning (1) you can't go to sleep as quickly and (2) your sleep is not as restful. The second effect is that the content you're viewing can affect your sleep in a negative way. This is especially true if you're watching the news or scrolling through social media. It becomes harder to calm your brain.

With devices like smartphones and tablets, the blue light from these devices reduces your melatonin production. Apple's iPhones and iPads now have a "Night Shift" mode designed to turn light more yellow, but that's really not good enough.

I typically tell my clients, "Put down the phone an hour before bed, and don't have a TV in the bedroom." Train yourself that when it's time for bed, it's time to shut everything down. If you want to read, read an actual book. Your bedroom should have softer light. Eating something a couple of hours before you go to bed and taking a warm bath or shower will also help you relax. You can also try listening to quiet music (make sure it's nothing that's going to amp you up). It's much easier for you to go to sleep because your body is already in a more soothed, calmer state by the time your head hits the pillow.

Another way to condition yourself for a great night's sleep: Don't do anything in your bedroom other than sleep, dress, and have sex. That way, you build associations with the physical environment you're in. Some of the worst things you could do in your bedroom would be to argue, do paperwork, or, even worse, pay bills. Those are the kind of negative associations that are going to seriously impact your ability to rest. Your subconscious doesn't really know that it's bedtime. All it does is associate with whatever you're usually doing in that physical space. Save that space for good stuff! It's about building a very clear boundary between the place where you sleep and the rest of the world.

Back to Basics: Take A Nap!

When it comes to napping, everyone is different. If you can tolerate it, a nap in the afternoon is a decent idea. It's a good practice if your body is feeling tired. If you are tired and you take a break, it teaches your body that it is okay to stop. It's *okay to sleep*.

A lot of people hit that point in the afternoon when they're dragging, and they push through it. They grab their afternoon coffee or energy drink and force their bodies to keep going. This teaches your body, "Nope. I know you're tired, but sleeping is not right. It's unsafe. It's not good. So let's just push through." When you go to bed at night, those same messages are going strong. It becomes harder for your body to relax into a state of rest, and you end up losing valuable sleep. You drink more coffee or energy drinks the next day – to make up for the sleep you missed last night – and the vicious cycle continues.

If you need a nap, you typically don't want to nap for longer than an hour or an hour-and-a-half. Also, try to make sure your nap is done by no later than three o'clock in the afternoon. Longer than that, or too late in the day, and it may screw up your sleep that night.

A lot of men have huge "sleep debts," and are only making minimum payments. If you can start to pay back that debt by napping in the afternoon, it will reduce some of the deficit. Sometimes, even fifteen minutes of closing your eyes and just resting can help regenerate your body and fill that void.

The Importance of Breaks

"Leisure" is a dirty word to many men, but we desperately need it. Taking breaks during the day helps reduce your arousal, which helps increase your performance. Anything you can do to create a soothing sensation in your body helps you get lower on the arousal scale and improve your performance.

I suggest that people set a timer that repeats every three hours. When you get up in the morning, eat some food, focus on being calm for one minute, and then hit your timer. When the alarm goes off in three hours, take a break, get a snack, and do it again. Do that throughout the day, and your physical health will benefit from taking sufficient breaks *and* addressing your nutrition, killing the proverbial two birds with one stone.

Take Mini-Vacations

After you eat, take a minute or two—or five if you can spare it—to just sit and be quiet. Look out the window, find something nice to look at, like some scenery, or close your eyes and imagine yourself on a beach. Or just feel your butt in the chair. Anything that will stop the normal flow of work, stress, or production, for that little bit of time. It makes your work time more efficient. I call these short breaks "mini-vacations."

Mini-vacations teach your body, similar to naps, that it's okay to *stop*. Most guys – people in general, but especially guys – just go, go, go, then fall down exhausted at the end of the day and think they're going to sleep well. It's the equivalent of driving your car down the highway at 100 mph and jamming it into park. It's not good for you, your car, or anybody around you. Don't do that to your body.

You can take your mini-vacations when you wake up, just before you go to sleep, or after each meal. Take a minute. Be quiet and just be still. Breathe. Let your food digest. Feel your ass in the chair, feel your feet on the floor. Notice how your breath moves.

When you take these breaks after your meals or at any other time during the day, your nervous system, your brain, and your subconscious understand that stopping is not the end of the world. Nothing bad happens, and it slows down your nervous system and your whole physiology. And, as already mentioned, when you go to bed at night, you already have a template for stopping, so it's much easier to fall asleep and get better-quality sleep as well.

Taking a little break helps your brain settle down and relax. Your whole physiology calms down, not only in the present but throughout the rest of your day, acting as a "stress firewall." Let's say your morning was stressful, and you take a mini-vacation during your coffee break. That break bleeds off some of the morning's stress. The stressful morning will not control the rest of your day or cause you to spiral into even more stressful things. Starting out stressed means you're more likely to make mistakes or piss people off because of your attitude.

Taking that mini-vacation when you begin to feel stressed can turn things around. It can provide the energy you need to tackle those bigger problems, especially if you practice taking mini vacations on a regular basis.

Relax and Take A Break

Being relaxed and calm is integral to learning, change, and higher-order thinking. Try to take just one minute, a few times a day, to relax. Here are one-minute relaxation techniques that you may find helpful:

Relaxation exercise #1: Close your eyes. Feel the weight of the chair beneath you; feel your body sinking deeper into your chair. Tell yourself that your body is becoming heavier and heavier. Just focus on the sensation of heaviness in your body. Breathe deeply and when you exhale, sink even deeper into that feeling of heaviness. Now bring your awareness back to the room and open your eyes.

Relaxation exercise #2: Pay attention to your breath. Put your hands on your stomach and inhale. Fill your stomach first, then your chest. Exhale. Inhale again, counting 1-2-3-4. Hold, counting 1-2-3-4. Exhale, counting 1-2-3-4. Repeat three times.

Relaxation exercise #3: Close your eyes and inhale deeply, fill your abdomen completely, then your chest, hum your best bass note as you let out the entire breath. Repeat three times. Sit silently for minute. Open your eyes.

How do you feel after relaxing for one minute? How does it feel compared to 15 minutes ago?

Chapter Six

The Emotional Factor: Why Men Are Bad at Expressing Emotions

There are three basic feelings we show as men: Hungry, Angry, and Horny. (Sometimes Happy - but only if our team wins.)

All joking aside, many of us do need a reminder that men are more than just a sum of those three emotions. The problem is, most of us were never taught that emotions of all kinds are okay. Many of us think of emotions as extensions of weakness.

Emotions are *good*. They're healthy. A lot of men simply have trouble with them.

Unfortunately, most of us have never been taught how to talk about our feelings. In fact, this is often cited as one of the reasons men tend to have shorter lifespans than women. We aren't taught to express and accept our emotions, whereas women have been socialized to talk about and deal with those emotions as they come up. Men are socialized to believe that emotions are somehow not manly, that feelings are "girly." But that's not true at all.

A lot of men won't show emotion with their spouse or their friends and family, but they'll show emotions at the football game. It's a perfect example of how confused we are on this issue. We *have* these emotions, but we don't always know how to express them in a healthy way.

Why Are Women Better at Expressing Themselves?

My psychologist puts it this way: most guys can generally throw a football a little bit better than most women can throw a football. That's not being sexist; it's just that guys typically grow up throwing more footballs than women do. On the other hand, women typically grow up talking about emotions more than men. As a result, most women are generally better at handling their emotions and expressing themselves.

Granted, there are some women who can throw a football better than most guys, and there are also some guys that are more in touch with their emotions than a great many women. The point is these things are not hardwired in us. They are *acquired* traits – learned skills that we can develop and improve upon.

We men sometimes function like little kids. Too much emotional intensity can feel overwhelming. That's just how our brains are set up. It puts us into fight-or-flight mode. This becomes a problem for couples, because the woman in the relationship is typically more comfortable with emotions than the man is. When too much is coming at him – even too much of a good thing – he shuts down (glossing over, thinking about something else, or focusing on media).

When it's fight or flight, most of us choose to flee. Of course, we also head for a fight a lot sooner when we feel threatened. This causes an "arms race" with our partner: We feel overwhelmed (again, even when its good stuff coming at us) so we withdraw emotionally. The loss of connection triggers her fight-

or-flight response so she pursues more intently to try to reconnect. This intensity scares us even more so we withdraw even more or put up a fight. And she pursues more. Pretty soon its Armageddon and neither of us know how we got there.

A friend of mine told me about an interview with General H. Norman Schwarzkopf, the man who was in charge of U.S. forces during the first Gulf War. Schwarzkopf was talking about when they were carpet-bombing in Iraq – how the enemy forces were running while the bombs came falling down on them – and he started to cry.

The interviewer said, "Stormin' Norman, you're crying. What's going on?"

General Schwarzkopf basically said, "These soldiers were fighting for what they thought was right too. They love their country and their children. The loss of life is sad. If a man can't show emotion, he's not really a man."

This is a tough general, a man who's in charge of killing people and running the military forces of the nation. What a beautiful example of the truth of a man's capacity for emotion.

It takes more toughness to be vulnerable and show your emotions than it does to pretend that everything's okay or that you don't have feelings. Gentleness, appreciation, sorrow, and sadness…these things take more courage to show than pretending you're King Shit.

A Word about Anger

One of the things men get in trouble for a lot is being angry. Honestly, it's kind of a double bind. If you don't have some kind of edge to your personality it's impossible to set boundaries and you get walked all over. On the other hand, walking around with a chip on your shoulder, pissed off and ready to fight, is not good either. The idea is *not* to find balance – there is no balance – but to remember the truth about anger and make it work for you.

First off, you're probably not actually a hothead. Most people blow up not because they want to be in adult tantrum mode all the time, but because they don't get angry soon enough. Here's what I mean: if you are too passive and try to "make nice" all the time you are negating your feelings all day long. You tell yourself something like "I don't want to ruin the good time we're having" or "It's really not that bad" or "Everyone says I'm too uptight all the time. I can't talk about this, it's too nit-picky" or, worse yet, "Just wait until he/she does that again – then they are really going to get it." We all reach a point where there is simply no more room in the "shit eating" container and we explode. At that stage, you look crazy because what you are reacting to is something relatively minor compared to the force it ends up spewing. If your default setting is sucking it up (you know – like a man) then you're basically walking around ready to explode at any moment.

Here's the truth about anger. It serves two purposes: it is an alarm and it is fuel. Anger comes up when your boundaries have been violated (even when you let them be violated or you do it to yourself by not filling your "Me" tank). It's also energy to do something about that violation. So when you pay attention to your feelings of anger you can ask yourself "Where do I feel that someone has stepped on my toes?" and then you can figure out the best way to address it – you will need the energy to confront someone or change your habits. Realize that sometimes we are the ones guilty of stepping on our own toes.

Here's how it played out for me: I grew up with a "rage-aholic" dad. He was always yelling at everyone and you never knew what would set him off. I never wanted to be like that. In fact, I was afraid of my anger because I thought it would destroy me and everyone around me if I let it out. So I became a pacifist. I figured I'd just be a peacemaker and suck things up (you know, because I was strong and I could take it). This only made matters worse. Once people saw that I would just laugh/shrug it off they came at me harder and more often. The rare time I did "let out the beast" it was pretty scary. This only confirmed my fears that I was ending up just like my old man.

By the time I was in university I was walking around with a stupid vacant smile on my face trying to be a nice guy while my friends used to laugh at me because my hands were always in fists. Secretly I wished someone would attack me or call me a "Nigger" so I would have a legitimate reason to finally unleash my anger and feel some relief. All along I was so dead inside that I really believed that I was a pacifist and had it all under control (Mr. Spock and Data were my patron saints – yes, I'm also a Trekkie.)

When I was in graduate school, there was a course involving psychological tests we would have to practice on one another. On every test I took my anger scale was always off the charts. I couldn't understand it (but my girlfriends could). Finally, when I started seeing a psychologist I was able to comprehend what was really going on and learn what I just shared with you (you get it for just the cost of this book).

So stop sucking it up and start addressing things when something bugs you.

Timing also counts. If you're driving down the highway and your engine starts to make weird noises, it's not a good idea to pull over and immediately start ripping your engine apart to fix the problem. Working on a hot engine will usually wreck it and definitely burn your hands. The same is true in any relationship. Yes, you need to address things that bug you, but wait until the engine cools. You'll have way more success at resolution and are less likely to get burned. When things are calm say, "Hey, can I talk to you about something that's been bugging me? I'm only bringing this up because I don't want it to fester and cause us problems later, when we are not looking. The other day when you said/did X I felt hurt/ pissed off/ scared/ frustrated/ confused/ etc." This is far less threatening and thus gives you a greater chance of success.

How to Connect with Your Emotions

The inability to identify or express emotions is a more common problem than you might realize. As I just explained, I actually had it myself. The technical term is alexithymia. It's basically frozen feelings, or "no words for feelings" – the inability to identify, talk about, and healthily express emotions.

A lot of guys, especially if they've grown up in a dysfunctional family or have been through trauma, are basically dead inside. Women can experience this, too. One of the things that I encourage men to do, first of all, is to start allowing themselves to *have* emotions. This is the first baby step toward *talking* about them.

GET A GOOD PSYCHOLOGIST

One of the processes that I went through, and that I'd recommend to anyone, is getting yourself a good psychologist. This can be scary for guys because you think it means something's wrong with you. But one of my mottoes is "Easier, Faster, Farther." If I can find a technique, resource or coach/mentor (in this case a psychologist) that can help me be more efficient and effective in my life, then I'd be an idiot NOT to use it. It's my advantage in the game of life, business, and success. Find somebody to help you walk through what you're dealing with and build the capacity to express your emotions. It really does add depth, joy, color, texture – everything – to life when you are able to feel. You are able to get in touch with your empathetic side, and people are able to feel empathy towards you.

When you're frozen inside – when you are that robot or that hyper-logical person – not only are you difficult to be around, but you don't get to enjoy the connections, the love, and the support that surrounds you. It can be a very lonely and unfulfilling life even when you have people around you. But if you just suck it up, suck it up, suck it up, and never talk it out, then in the end you will explode.

That's when people act out in rage or violence, or just come across as assholes in general. Inside, the person might feel that they are not an angry person, but they come across as angry because the only time anything ever comes out is when it's overflowing like a volcano.

FIND YOUR TEAM

Get with somebody who can help you express yourself. Have good friends. Find people who are safe and let them know that you're working on things. People who are in a good place will be happy to help work through this with you. Talk about what's going on in men's groups, with other friends, with one close friend, or, better yet, with your spouse or partner. I'm in a mastermind group with two other men. We meet once a month and hold each other's feet to the fire while sharing our successes and our frustrations.

WRITE DOWN YOUR FEELINGS

If talking to people is too difficult at first, start by writing your feelings out just to begin to identify what your emotions are.

This will help you recognize that you do have feelings and you're not a one-dimensional person.

HAVE FUN!

Building happy experiences into your life also helps. Include adventures and people in your life that give you positive emotions. Look for things that are fun.

A lot of guys are so geared toward being practical that we won't take time for pleasing activities – to play or to do things that are joyful. Instead, we always try to be practical. "Well no, I don't have time for that. I've got to mow the lawn," or "I have to pay the bills," or "I can't today, I have to do [fill in the blank]."

Fun could be shooting some hoops, fishing, hunting, a guys' weekend, or getting away on vacation. We end up getting depleted because we don't add any of the positive emotional experiences into our lives. Remember the earlier example of the adult day care center? It's important to look after that dimension and remember to just have fun sometimes.

Think about balance scales (like the scales of justice). If you have a ton of stress and negativity on one side and you want to be in better balance, you either have to remove some stress from one side (not always possible) or add positive stuff to the other side.

Let your Brain Breathe in Solitude

Solitude is vital to your emotional well-being. Make some time for solitude every so often – ideally every day. As adults, in particular, we only get to process and integrate new material by having solitude and quiet time. If you're too busy, or the radio is always playing in the car, or you're always checking your phone, or the TV is always on in the background, you never really have a chance to process new material. We don't get the chance to do the necessary assessment to see if life is working for us or not.

A friend of mine does a solitude activity every so often where he goes to a silent retreat. He goes any time he has to make a major decision or is facing a particularly challenging or life-changing situation. He will spend three to seven days in silence and just be with himself, with his own thoughts. As a result, he is able to express his emotions and gain clarity about whatever decision or situation he is there to deal with.

Turn off the distractions and let your brain breathe.

Don't Chase the Snake: Forgive and Let Go

One of the things that can help you to be emotionally healthy is the concept of forgiveness and letting go. There is a common misunderstanding about what forgiveness is. Forgiveness is not, "Hey, that was fun. Let's do that again." Forgiveness is not, "It's okay that you hurt me." Forgiveness is for the person *doing* the forgiving, not the person being forgiven. It's your way to let go – deciding not to carry resentment and anger around with you. Holding on to resentment or trying to get even is like holding acid in your mouth, hoping you'll someday get a chance to spit it on your enemy; it will burn you more than it burns them, and you may never get a chance to spit it out.

What would you do if a poisonous snake bit you? You could stop, administer first aid, and try to get to a hospital and survive. Or you could be pissed off with the snake and go and chase it through the bush trying to kill it. The second option doesn't work very well, but we do that all the time in our lives. We chase the snake. Something happens, and we obsess over the cause of it. We carry it around with us. It becomes part of our identity.

Some people actually look forward to their opportunity to be toxic toward the person responsible. They are pissed off all day and can't wait to see them. For some of us, that person becomes our kryptonite. We're in a good mood all day, only to show up at a party, and as soon as we see that person, our faces twist up, there is a knot in our stomach, and we feel angry again. They may never even know we're there! Who does that really hurt? Don't chase the snake. Learn to forgive and let go.

HOW TO APOLOGIZE

By forgiving and letting go, we also open ourselves up to be able to apologize sincerely when something is *our* fault. When you say you're sorry, you get to forgive yourself. You get to take responsibility for how your actions impacted the other person in a negative way. Whether you meant something to hurt or not, if you hurt the other person according to their definition (and if they feel hurt they *are* hurt; you don't get to rule whether they are "really" hurt), you need to take responsibility for that and apologize. This ultimately frees you up.

Whether the other person forgives you or not, you must do what you need to do to take responsibility. That makes you a stronger, healthier person, which also contributes towards building your self-esteem.

Men tend to think that apologizing shows weakness, but people respect men who can own their shit far more than people who deny it or pretend it's somebody else's fault. Be responsible and own up to your stuff. That is strength.

Weakness vs. Strength

I hold a black belt in karate and am currently learning Aikido. Aikido is considered a "weak art," or strength through weakness, because Aikido is a yielding type of force. When force is coming at you, you yield to it. You absorb the force and redirect it for your own purposes. In order to be strong, you have to be weak first. I think that's a wonderful analogy for what real strength is.

The traditional way a guy has been taught to see strength is to be rock hard. Unyielding. It's the cowboy riding off into the sunset by himself, the superhero handling everything, taking the whole world on his shoulders and never showing any emotion. But that's not strength.

First of all, that definition of strength is a fantasy. It's made up. Real strength is based in being vulnerable. Real strength is being kind, being generous, and being able to express your feelings – joy, sadness, and fear.

We all feel the same emotions. No one is immune to fear. One of the things my dad used to say to me all the time is that "the only difference between a hero and a coward is the direction in which they run." Courage is facing something head-on, dealing with it and not running away. Courage is not the absence of fear. It is action in spite of fear or in the face of fear, taking into account all your feelings and choosing to act anyway.

We don't have to be this solid-rock, untouchable, unmovable person. We can feel pain, joy, sadness, and fear. What counts is what we do with it, what we do with what we have, and if we stick with our goals. Can we do that and still show kindness, affection, and all our other emotions? That's what makes a person strong.

Aikido is also called "the lazy martial art" because the effort expended to apply the technique is minimal. This is also a great analogy for life, relationships, communication and conflict. My Sensei was explaining this concept and a technique he was teaching us. He said it this way:

> *Let's say it's your anniversary and your wife has cooked this wonderful meal, she's got the candles out, and she is wearing a nice outfit. You are about to leave work and head home,*

but your boss says, "Hey, you can't go. There is an emergency. You've got to stay here and help." The problem is, your phone is dead, and you can't get to a phone to let your wife know what's going on.

You show up three hours late. All the candles are burned down. The food is cold. You come into the house, and she is furious. You can choose to be angry right back at her and say, "What else could I do? I had to work! I couldn't help it!" You get into a fight and ruin your anniversary.

Or you can choose to yield. You can say, "You know what? I'm so sorry. Look at all the stuff you did. You look so nice. Dinner looks delicious. I'm so sorry I missed it."

She might still be angry for a while, but she'll calm down. She'll soften because you are listening to her. You are acknowledging and validating her feelings. Once she knows you're listening to her and she has calmed down, then you can say, "I'm really sorry. Is it okay if I tell you what happened with me? Here's what was happening with me at work."

All of a sudden, you are communicating. You are supporting each other. You can have a really nice anniversary with each other. Things may not have gone exactly the way you wanted them to, but you're still connected.

To me, that's real strength.

Chapter Seven

The Intellectual, Spiritual, and Financial Factors

"If you will improve, be content to be thought stupid and a fool."

EPICTETUS, GREEK PHILOSOPHER

Humans are built to learn continuously. It's in our biology. The problem is, many people don't like to feel foolish or look stupid and so they tend not to try new things. They stick only to what they are good at. Maybe you are one of those people.

The problem with this approach to life is that, over time, your life gets smaller and smaller, it diminishes as you age. The more active your brain is, the healthier it will be.[11] The longer your brain stays functional, the more you can ward off what we used to think of as age-related mental decline. This can be done by staying active, not just physically but mentally – taking a new class, learning a new language, starting a different hobby, traveling to new places, having experiences you have never had before.

Above all, try something you are not very good at. Again, most men tend to stick to what we're good at because we don't want to feel stupid or look incompetent. Get past that fear. Look for those things that are difficult for you or that you've never tried before but have always wanted to try. If we stick only with what we know and what is already going well for us, we get bored. Learning a new skill stimulates your brain and keeps it strong.

The novelty of new experiences, physiologically, *forces* your brain to grow stronger: it causes more dendrite generation, leading to increased serotonin. You also get all the other healthy brain chemicals that make you smart, sharp, and happy. You sleep better and, of course, you also get the feeling of satisfaction from learning a new task or skill or just from trying something new.

I mentioned in the previous chapter that I started doing Aikido. Despite the fact that I had been practicing karate for years, Aikido was a brand new experience for me. It hit my Intellectual Me Factor because of its novelty. Whereas karate is considered a "hard and direct" technique, moving in straight lines, I had to learn to be flexible in Aikido. It challenged me in new ways, and men thrive on challenges.

Trying something new is also a great remedy for depression or burnout, especially when there isn't too much at stake – something you can do for fun. There are multiple apps available now, such as Brain Gym, which can help your brain stay sharp and active. My wife loves to do Sudoku. Any kind of puzzle or test is great for helping you keep sharp.

Most universities let you audit classes, or you can take a course at a community college. Take an online course in something that interests you. Again, look for novelty. Keep your brain exercising. Look for new experiences and make the search a priority.

Music is a very helpful and often overlooked way of keeping the mind active. Listening to music is a good start, but playing music, singing, or dancing tend to be more effective at expanding your brain and helping it grow. Musicians tend to have a much lower incidence of Alzheimer's and dementia, apparently because they use their brains differently.[12] If you don't play an instrument, wouldn't it be great to learn? Try taking a class and see what happens.

It takes guts to step out and try something new. It can feel downright uncomfortable. But new experiences are essential to your intellectual well-being.

Spiritual

Men have a tendency to want to speed through everything: work, meals, emotions, and sex. But you can't speed through spirituality.

Throughout human history, there has always been some form of spirituality, whether that means shamanism, polytheism, Judaism, Christianity, Islam, other belief systems, or even atheism. But when I say "spirituality," I'm not necessarily talking about religion.

Spirituality is bigger than religion; it's a sense of recognition of something greater than yourself. Native American writer Vine Deloria Jr. captures the essence of the difference between religion and spirituality: "Religion is for people who are afraid of going to hell. Spirituality is for those who have already been there."

Spirituality is a human need. Although our modern culture has changed and we may not be subscribing to religion to understand our physical world as we have in the past, it does not mean the spiritual dimension has left us. To be effective, efficient, and healthy, we have to recognize that need and fill it.

Spirituality used to come to us naturally. In more primitive societies, communing with nature, and with one other, and taking the time to appreciate things – spirituality – was all around us. Now, we have to be deliberate about it. We have to actively slow down.

For men, that doesn't always mean going to church, synagogue, mosque or a physical place of worship. It could be having a sense of appreciation for the things around you. It might mean taking the time to pause for a moment and "come to your senses", like smelling the air when you walk from your car to the office building. "Stop and smell the roses" is the old cliché, but anytime you take the time to slow down and notice the subtler aspects of life, you are feeding your Spiritual Me Factor.

The next time you are taking a shower, take a moment to feel the water on your skin, feel the warmth and the wetness... smell the soap or the shampoo. Any break from your practical routine to become present with your senses can be a spiritual awakening.

Tasting your food – really tasting your food and paying attention to the flavor, aroma, texture, and temperature – can be a spiritual act. Taking the time to chew slowly and savor the love that went into preparing the meal or appreciating the person who prepared the meal is a quick way to bring you back to what is important in your life. It can be as simple as taking a walk in a forest. It could be going to the museum. Appreciating a piece of art or a well-designed muscle car. It might just mean being in the moment while you're having sex. It's something that feeds your soul and your spirit.

Spirituality is a transcendent experience of living. Things like meditation, yoga, mindfulness, prayer, and journaling all contribute to putting us in that state. But really, any time we show appreciation and take time to acknowledge, be thankful, and truly appreciate anything, what we're really doing is getting in contact with our spiritual selves.

Journaling

Journaling meets the need for both the Emotional and Spiritual Me Factors (can be Intellectual too). When you take the time to journal, you are spending time with yourself; you are writing about yourself, for yourself, and that, to me, makes it a spiritual experience.

I wasn't always a believer in journaling. My psychologist told me about journaling early in my adult life, but back then I didn't believe her because...well, because I'm a guy, right? "Journaling? Really? Yeah, I don't need that. It's emotions. Why do I need those?"

This went on for about two years. She kept suggesting it, and I kept fighting her on it. I was going to see her every week. Every week she'd ask me about it, and every week I'd say, "No, no, I do not do that." But finally, after two years, I started to journal, and journaling, as it turned out, was incredibly helpful. I had to concede: "Oh. Okay. This is what she was talking about. I get it now."

Journaling helped me with everything I was working on with my psychologist at the time and really accelerated my progress. Not only that, but it helped me with my relationship, my job, and my mental state. I felt better physically when I started journaling because it was a way of externalizing all the emotions that I usually let build up inside.

People are typically better on *all* measures when they journal because it is a tool for self-awareness. I now journal regularly, and it is a spiritual exercise for me. If I journal in the morning, I know I've done something for myself. I have addressed those

Me Factors right off the bat, first thing in the morning, and that feeds me emotionally, spiritually, and intellectually and starts my day off on the right foot.

Journaling requires slowing down. It requires a time commitment but can be as little as a 5-minute commitment, ideally daily. During your journaling time, it's the only thing you should be doing. You shouldn't be journaling while watching TV or trying to carry on a conversation. Pick a time and place where you have privacy and will not be disturbed. Also lock away your journal or hide it. You want to be free to fully express your thoughts and feelings without editing yourself. Focus on the writing. It is an opportunity to practice self-reflection, appreciation, and honoring your emotions. You'll discover hidden insights about what you've learned and where you want to go. I keep my journals and look back to remind myself of things I've discovered (sometimes I forget) and to see how far I've come or where I might still be stuck.

Journaling feeds your soul. It also helps you cope with tough times. When I was finishing my doctorate, I was living in Fort McMurray, Alberta, so I flew down to Michigan where I went to school. I sat down with my dissertation committee, and they gave me feedback.

I had been working on my dissertation for more than seven years at this point. It was 250 pages long, and they were asking me to make certain changes. I said, "No problem." This was before laptops and flash drives, so I went to the computer lab with my floppy disk and inserted it in the drive. My version of the software was so far behind that it updated to the new version, and in an instant, the formatting of the entire document was gone.

Picture 250 pages of text—about half of it tables full of data—with all the formatting gone. It was just one straight line of text, running through the whole document. The reality slowly sank in. I was going to have to go through and recreate all the tables and redo all the formatting, one item at a time.

I only had a limited amount of time because I had to fly back home. Graduation was coming, and I had exhausted all my extensions already. On top that, one of my committee members had told me she didn't like a lot of my references and wasn't going to pass me. She hadn't bothered to tell me this at any point during this entire process but instead decided to tell me right at the end.

To say I was stressed would be putting it lightly. I was freaking out. I was panicking.

I went to the bookstore, bought a notebook, and started writing how I felt. I wrote about how panicked I was and how my guts were in knots. Then I wrote out all the fears I had about not graduating, how embarrassing it would be, what it was going to cost me, and how disappointed everybody would be. I had to get it all out.

Writing all this down externalized the experience for me. At that point, I was able to calm down, go to the lab, buckle down, and do what I needed to do to get my dissertation back in order.

At that chaotic time, I was probably writing in my journal three to five times a day every day, just to have a place to put all the stress and anxiety. Otherwise, the stress would have been constant, without any reprieve, and I would not have been able to sleep at night. I would have been too panicked to get anything done. Journaling really helped me in that instance, and that is one of the reasons I am such a big believer in it.

Spirituality in an Unspiritual World

Spirituality, in general, is a celebration. It is the process of taking time to observe, acknowledge, and honor our own progress and our place in the universe.

The concept of celebrating accomplishments and milestones has been part of human culture for as long as culture has existed, but for some reason we have gotten away from it. We do not give ourselves nearly enough credit. We do not take the time to feel and experience how well we are doing. By not taking the time to see the good coming from the environment, or taking time for ourselves, we feel tired, burned out, and negative.

I have found that martial arts can be quite spiritual once you understand the concepts and traditions. Getting out in nature is also an important spiritual exercise, particularly with current advancements in technology. I recently took a trip into the wilderness. Being around ancient trees and 300-million-year-old mountains gave me perspective and a sense of awe and reverence.

Think about the speed of our culture today versus one hundred years ago. This is the first time in modern history that we're getting so much information so quickly, every day. I recently heard an estimate that a single edition of the *New York Times* has more information than people got in an entire lifetime a few hundred years ago. We are getting that, and more, daily – we are bombarded with information.

The case against technology is only getting stronger. Studies show that the more time kids spend staring at screens, the more depressed and anxious they become. [13] They also do worse in school and are meaner to their friends and family members. But when kids go outside and play, the trend reverses. They exhibit much more happiness, compassion, and patience. They are simply happier.

Thought Experiments

One of the tools Albert Einstein used in the development of his theory of relativity was "thought experiments." Basically, Einstein would sit down and think about an outcome. Then he'd think about the logical consequences of those outcomes. One thing would lead to the next, all within his mind, and through this process he came up with an entirely new system of physics and astronomy on which we have built modern-day life.

That sounds a bit like mediation. You might almost call it spiritual.

Here's a thought experiment for you. Imagine yourself well fed, well-rested, energized, and happy. Maybe you've just gotten back from vacation. Think about how you would feel, how happy you would be, what your body would feel like. As you do this, write down how you feel. Follow the progression. What kind of husband would you be if you always felt that way? What kind of father would you be? Friend? Worker? What kind of man would you be?

By seeing those outcomes, you're visualizing the person you want to become.

Financial

Finances are often a touchy and emotional subject. I've had accountants and investment advisers tell me that people confide things to them that they don't even tell their spouse – which is frightening. It has become one of these weird areas where it's clearly important and we know we need to talk about it, but we don't.

The American Psychological Association continues to find that money is one of the top causes of stress for individuals. [14] It is also the #1 cause of tension in relationships. In other words, if you can get a handle on your money, you're knocking off a top cause of stress in your individual life *and* the #1 cause of stress in your relationship. How huge is that?

Clearly, your financial well-being is important if you're going to live a balanced life. If you don't have some basic financial understanding, at least – if not financial security – it makes life much harder.

You may be familiar with Maslow's Hierarchy of Needs, a pyramid of human requirements for healthy living. The bottom, the base, is comprised of physiological needs and general safety – survival stuff like shelter and food and warmth. At the top is what they call "self-actualization," which is expressing yourself and feeling good, living to your full potential. There's a reason that category is at the top. Feeling warm and fulfilled just isn't a priority if the basic necessities of life like food and shelter aren't taken care of first. Whether you're a corporate raider or a vegan hippie, we all need a certain level of infrastructure in order to *survive* before we can move beyond and *thrive*.

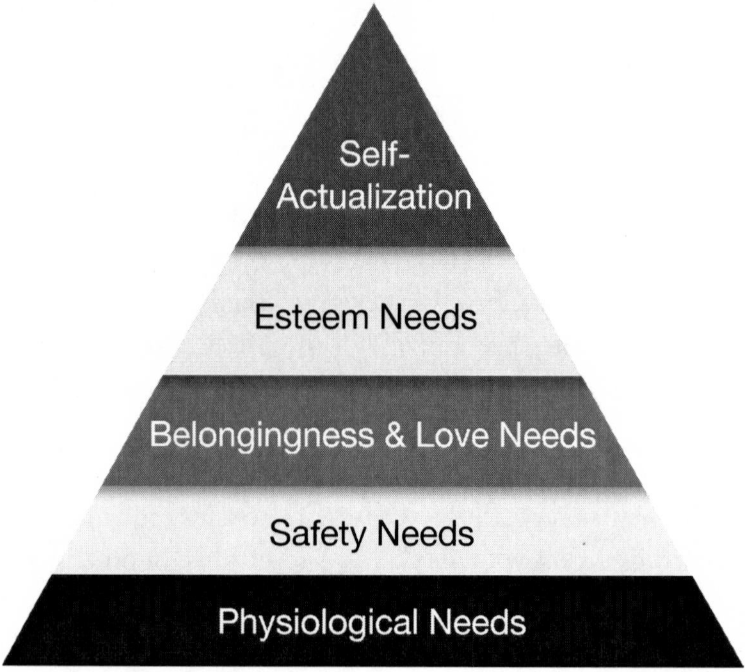

Recreated from simplypsychology.org

©Copyright 2018 Dr. Ganz Ferrance

In our culture, money is like air. For better or worse, that's just how it is. Without money, your choices are limited. If you *really* don't have it, it's akin to living with the threat of violence or abuse; you've got to get that taken care of in order to have fulfillment and the productivity.

When I was younger, I would make investments and think, *If I just made a lot of money, I would be secure.* But really, it's the other way around. It starts by taking care of your security needs, making sure you have some extra money saved as an emergency fund – or a contingency fund, as I like to call it. Then, you can worry about making extra money.

After you have your "insurance" in place – so that you're covered in case you get sick or something happens to you or your property – it's a lot easier to invest in additional financial ventures because you know you have a buffer. Trying to make money quickly or start a business quickly or attempt any other high-risk activities where your livelihood and your family's well-being is riding on its success causes a lot of stress. Your emotions are likely to get the better of you and skew your decisions when so much is at stake.

I know what you're probably saying, "Hold up. Didn't Dr. Ganz just spend an entire chapter telling me that emotions are *good*?" Yes. But finances are the exception.

Finances require a degree of objectivity. The more emotional you are when it comes to money, the less clear you are, which sets you up to make bad choices, which can be a recipe for disaster. It starts a chain reaction. Worry sets in. Then panic. You can't sleep at night.

Most poor financial choices can be traced back to being stressed about money! If you know you've got a plan and you've taken care of the basics first, it's easier to be more thoughtful about how to make it to the next level, whatever that might be for you. But that doesn't mean pinching every penny. Treat yourself once in a while! Why else are you working, anyway?

Money is a tool to reach your goals; it's not the goal itself. Give yourself something to look forward to. If you deprive yourself, chances are it will result in an unhealthy binge later anyway.

Educate Yourself

I strongly recommend taking the time to educate yourself about finances, not just about which things to invest in or how certain securities work but about the proper mindset regarding money. There are innumerable books that can help you wrap your head around your finances. Suze Orman, for example, offers tips on managing finances and the money mindset. I like Robert Kiyosaki, as well. His book *Rich Dad, Poor Dad* is a foundational guide to investing and he also talks about how to adopt a money mindset.

Have a Money Plan

Financial well-being is an essential part of our day-to-day lives. Regardless of how much money you have in the bank, if you don't feel like you have a solid handle on your finances, you will feel stressed.

Talk with friends, go to seminars, consult financial advisers and people you trust – qualified people, not your plumber. You don't have to do it alone, but you do have to make sure that the people you are listening to are qualified and know what they are talking about, and that you feel a sense of trust and integrity when you are dealing with them.

Have a "spending plan" (this used to be called a budget). When you have a good financial spending plan and you're able to put money away, you know you are saving either for retirement, that trip you want to take, or that major purchase. But you also know you have enough to cover any life issues that might come up.

Make sure you know how to balance your checkbook and access your accounts online. These basic skills will help you feel like you're financially literate, which helps you feel calmer and opens you up to far more success. You can start making more money and strengthening your relationships with your spouse, your family, and yourself. For some of us there's so much emotion around money that it seems overwhelming to deal with. This is actually quite common because money matters are so emotionally charged.

This is another place a good psychologist can help. You don't have to remain a hostage of your emotions. You are not alone.

Chapter Eight

The Social Factor

One of the reasons we have survived as a species for this long is that we don't do it by ourselves. We can't. We need other people.

Humans belong in groups. We're herd animals, which means we need social connection. Social isolation is very stressful and can lead to depression. When psychologists assess clients who have something going wrong in their lives, one of the first things we look at is their social support structure. We need to determine:

- Are they connected with family?
- Do they have friends?
- How often do they connect with other people?
- How well connected are they at their job?

Those things all make a difference in how well people do in general and, if they are having problems, how quickly they can get over those problems.

With the explosion of technology and social media, humans are now more broadly connected than at any other time in history. However, we're also less deeply connected. You can have thousands of friends on Facebook or even tens of thousands of followers on Twitter, and still feel lonely. On paper, it looks like we are well connected. This means that in addition to feeling lonely, we may also feel confused as to *why* we feel lonely.

One of the reasons for increased loneliness in the digital age is that we are not having one-on-one, live conversations with people as much as we used to. The option to "connect" over some kind of electronic format is often more convenient. But electronic contacts don't generate the feeling of being deeply connected. There's something missing – something that's been part of our growth, development, and evolution since long before we could even understand it.

I recommend you connect with somebody, in person, at least once a day. The quantity of connections is important, but it also matters *with whom* you connect. It is important to be discerning when pursuing social contact. You want to connect with the right people. There's an old saying attributed to Benjamin Franklin: "If you lie down with dogs, you get up with fleas." That's the truth! Be cautious of the company you keep.

Author and renowned businessman Jim Rohn famously said that we are the average of the five people we spend the most time with. We are greatly influenced – whether we like it or not – by those closest to us. It affects our way of thinking, our self-esteem, and our decisions.

The level of connection we share with the humans around us is incredible, so make sure you are connecting with uplifting, supportive, kind, and generous people. You do not want "frenemies." You want people who will support and share your values. You also want people with different viewpoints, because outside input and challenges to our assumptions help us grow as people.

Social Connections and Human Physiology

Our social life affects the quality of our long-term health and happiness. In fact, there are neurons in our brain called mirror neurons whose whole job is to mirror our environment. These neurons fire both when we perform an act *and* when we see the act being performed by someone else. They are especially strong in children's brains. (Hence the problem with the phrase, "Do as I say, not as I do.")

When kids are around their parents, they see their environment through their parents' eyes and learn through their actions. They learn how to be social, what to say, how to respond in different circumstances, and how to do life by watching their parents. As adults, mirror neurons still function, so if we are around negative, unhappy, or angry people, we will mirror them and tend to feel angry, miserable, and unhappy. After social interactions, consider taking the time to ask yourself:

- Is this person healthy for me to be around?
- Do I feel better when I'm with this person?
- Do I feel better when this person leaves?
- Do I feel drained when I think about interacting with this person, even over a phone call?

These questions add up to one large question: "Is this (relationship) working for me?"

Often, after reflecting on these questions, people find that old relationships need to be limited if not pruned entirely in order for them to stay happy.

Cut off Toxic Relationships – "Prune" Your Tree

Pruning is an interesting concept. When you prune a tree, you remove the dead branches. Especially for fruit trees, it involves shaping the tree to make it easier to harvest the fruit, and removing suckers (young branches) that are not growing in productive places so they do not take energy from the tree. This is a principle of life. When you start pruning the unhealthy aspects of your life, especially negative social relationships, you feel better. You grow as a person, and good fruit is produced.

Here's the deal: You are allowed to protect yourself. I often say to my clients, "Everybody deserves love, but some people deserve love from a safe distance!" You don't have to allow yourself to be marinated in a family member's toxicity to show them love and acceptance. You can accept them and love them, but you may need to limit your contact. Your love for them should arrive in the mailbox.

I like to say that you have to be your own Environmental Protection Agency. You have to protect your environment of success, so make sure you watch who and what is around you and part of your social connections.

Stress, anxiety, and other negative emotions are contagious. But this is not as simple as "feeling drained" after a social visit. Negative emotions literally have a physiological effect on your body. Put yourself in a negative environment with negative experiences, and your biology is negatively affected. Your immune system gets taxed. Stress hormones flood your body. Your heart has to work harder. That's why the long-term effects of chronic stress are so detrimental. It's bad enough to experience a one-time effect, but the cumulative effects can be exceptionally stressful.

Watch for negative behavior in the people you surround yourself with. Don't allow yourself to be manipulated, either. And do not let loyalty cloud your vision. Even if you have been friends with someone since kindergarten or you have known a certain a family member since birth, you can still limit your time spent with them; you can choose to keep them at a distance. If they are unhealthy and things can't be addressed or changed, it's okay to end the relationship or at least limit your contact with them. Give yourself permission to see them once a year, once a quarter, or once every five years: whatever you need. When you limit your contact, you can actually have a better relationship.

Bottom line; don't let people treat you badly. No matter who they are, you have the right to protect yourself, and it's not enough to say it. You have to do something to back up what you say. You have the right to put up healthy boundaries. In most cases no relationship is better than a bad relationship.

Follow Your Gut

There's a movie I love called *Leap of Faith*, in which Steve Martin plays a traveling evangelist who puts on fraudulent faith-healing revivals to make money. His character is kind of a clown, but there is one line that has become a mantra for my life. The scene starts with a young local kid in a small town where Steve Martin's character's bus breaks down. The kid is talking about following his dad's legacy. He would like to do something different, but he just can't; it's just what he has to do. Steve Martin replies, "I stick with what I *want* to do. It's a tough policy, but it works for me."

This might seem like a throwaway line, but it is a strong statement. It's true. It really is tough to go with your gut and do what works for you. Doing only what you want is extremely hard, but it works.

One example of a time when I didn't follow my gut was in my early twenties. There was this girl, we will call her Cheryl, who was always just kind of around. She liked me, and our families were close, but I had never really had much interest in her.

Any time things weren't going Cheryl's way, she would do something to get attention. I remember one time we got together to watch a movie with our friends, and she was moping and sulking and pouting. It made the whole evening miserable and uncomfortable for everyone. I learned later that someone finally asked her, "What's wrong?" She answered, "Ganz isn't paying any attention to me. You know, I don't think he likes me. I don't know what's wrong with me. I don't know why he isn't interested."

My friends kept coming to me and asking, "Why don't you go out with Cheryl? What's wrong with you? She's a good girl." One day, with my entire family around – mom, sister, friends, everybody – one of my friends said, "Why don't you just go out with Cheryl? It'll be great!" My whole family agreed.

There was a lot of external tension placed on me to go out with Cheryl. And it worked. I asked Cheryl out, and it ended up being a huge mistake.

At the time, I was trying to do the right thing. The right thing would have been to just not ask her out, but I couldn't do that because I was young and not emotionally mature enough to stand up to my family and friends. I was also a people-pleaser and a peacekeeper. I gave in to everybody else pushing me in that direction. The relationship caused me a lot of pain. It caused Cheryl a lot of pain, too. Not only was I was unhappy, but I was depressed. I had recurring stomach problems. My body was reacting physically because I knew it was not a good relationship.

I kept trying to make the relationship work because, on paper, she was a great fit. Good family, good-looking, hardworking, and she liked me. Our families got along well. It was easy for everybody else, but it wasn't a good fit for me.

Eventually, things ended in a horrible breakup, and she was really upset. She ended up stalking me for two years. Even after I moved on and got married, she made our life hell and terrorized my wife. This all could have been avoided if I had just followed my gut.

Instead of manning up and saying "no" or setting a boundary or explaining why I didn't even like being around Cheryl, I said, "Okay." Our personalities didn't match and I wasn't as attracted to her as I needed to be. And not just that: I didn't like certain aspects of her character. Yet I let other people choose what was right for me instead of choosing for myself.

Do What's Right for You

My experience with Cheryl was one of the reasons I developed The Me Factor system. I wanted to prevent this sort of situation from ever happening to me again, and I wanted to teach other men how to avoid the kind of pain it caused.

If I had been true to myself, I would never have gone out with this girl. I would have told her directly that we just weren't a good fit for one another. And while it may have hurt initially, it wouldn't have been to the extent and depth that I eventually hurt her. My wife and I would have been spared the frustration and aggravation that followed, and everybody would have been better off if I had just stuck to my guns and done what was right for me in the first place.

The moral of the story is that the right thing is often the hard thing, and this is one of the main messages I want you to get from this book: doing this work is not for the faint of heart.

What I am teaching is not the punk's way out. This is hard work. You've got to be tough to do what's right for you, but if you've got the guts, everybody wins.

So, what does it look like to do what's right? When I was younger, we had this old piano. It used to go out of tune all the time, so we would have to get the professional piano tuner to come in. In those days, tuning forks were used to match the pitch of the note. The tuner would hit the tuning fork, producing a perfect note, and adjust the strings on the piano until they resonated and matched the frequency of the tuning fork. That's how you knew the piano was in tune.

We all have our own internal tuning forks. You know what works and what doesn't work for you – when you pay attention, that is. If you're being treated well, it resonates. That's also how we recognize truth. It resonates with us.

Following your own tuning fork means following your gut. In relationships, if you're listening to your gut and you're present, you will know whether someone you are with is safe or unsafe.

Let me also note that the problem may not be in you or in the other person; it might just be the truth of the relationship, the interaction of two people, or the dynamic that exists between them. I've worked with couples where they are both good people, but, for whatever reason, when they are together they become poisonous to one another. It's not either person's fault. It's just that the interaction does not work well. This can happen with friendships, families, coworkers, or in any relationship.

You can get along with most people; some people, less so.

"No" Is a Complete Sentence

In Chapter Two, we talked about the importance of boundaries and the different types of boundaries. But what happens to a man who has no boundaries?

Men with no boundaries get *used.*

They get abused and used to death – literally. They're always trying to please people, and it slowly kills them.

In self-defense classes – especially women's self-defense – they teach students to say, "No!" Even as you're defending yourself and beating somebody up, you're instructed to keep saying, "No!", over and over again. This is because it gets you in touch with your own power. To teach this concept to my students, I do a "no" exercise in my workshops where people hammer you with requests and questions over and over again. Your job is to keep saying "no," just so you get used to it. It's empowering, and people find it very beneficial.

Of course, that's just a starting place. The real power is in knowing that it is your *right* to live your life and do what you want to do with your time. No one gets to tell you how to do that.

"No" really is a form of self-defense. I encourage you to practice saying it. It's like practicing free throws. You're not going to shoot foul shots through a whole basketball game, but when it does come time, and the pressure is on, you had better hope you practiced your shot.

I was presenting a workshop once about how to have boundaries in business and be successful, and one of the participants shared with the group how she had learned that "No" is a complete sentence. And I thought, *Yes! She's right. It is!*

"No" is all you are obligated to say. You do not have to explain yourself, you do not have to make excuses. You do not have to justify your unwillingness to do what someone is asking you to do. You are allowed to say "no" without giving a reason. It's your time, it's your energy, it's your life. You don't have to do something just because somebody asked nicely or keeps asking. You can't help them unless you can help yourself, so it is more responsible for you to say "no" sometimes. You always have the option to give an explanation, but remember, you don't *have* to explain yourself to anyone.

If you are incapable of saying "no", your "yes" ceases to mean anything. Your "yes" means nothing if that is always your response. This is how well-meaning men get trampled on and taken advantage of. And keep in mind, when you say "yes" to everything asked of you, you're saying "no" to other things by default. Usually, it is yourself, your health, your well-being, a date with your wife, time with your kids, a workout, or an hour more sleep.

I don't want to undersell or oversell this notion. It's hard work to say "no." It's hard to change those patterns of being everything for everybody or being the "go-to guy." And you know what? Even though it feels awful to have all that pressure on you sometimes, many of us thrive on it. You get praise for it. "Oh, thank you so much. You are amazing. You have never let me down. I can always count on you. You are incredible." You get all this self-worth validation and acknowledgment, so it can be really difficult to start saying, "No, I can't do that for you."

Assertiveness

If there's one central theme to The Me Factor System, it is that we all have needs. Our needs are real and legitimate, and we need to prioritize them.

There are four ways to fulfill our needs: We can be aggressive, passive, passive-aggressive, or assertive.

AGGRESSIVE

The aggressive person gets their needs fulfilled at all costs, and it doesn't matter whom they hurt to get that done. They will step over you and through you to get what they want. They don't care.

The aggressive approach is unhealthy and dysfunctional.

PASSIVE

There's a saying in the psychology world: "The opposite of dysfunction is dysfunction." In this case, the other extreme is to become passive, which isn't much better in terms of results. A passive person needs to have their needs met like anyone else, but they let people step all over them. They are the "go-to guy" described in the previous section. "I'm going to try to do everything I can to support you because I'm hoping you will either feel sorry for me or guilty enough that you will then fill my needs."

This is clearly not a good approach (and it's kind of weak and manipulative at the same time).

PASSIVE-AGGRESSIVE

A twist on passive behavior is the person who becomes passive-aggressive. They aren't content to be passive but fear being aggressive. The passive-aggressive person is nice to you to your face, and then scrubs the toilet with your toothbrush when you're not looking. In other words, when there's an issue, they won't do the constructive thing and come to you or try to solve the problem. They'll instead try to get back at you in a way you may not even be aware of, or they'll try to subtly manipulate you to get what they want.

You don't want to be that guy.

ASSERTIVE

An assertive person is somebody who recognizes they have needs and meets them in a way that does not interfere with anybody else meeting their needs. If they are really enlightened, they can meet their needs while also helping others meet their needs in a healthy way.

Being assertive is the wisest and healthiest way to meet your needs. An assertive person will ask for what they want but will also be willing to take "no" for an answer. An assertive person won't manipulate or coerce or threaten in order to get what they want. Assertive people are able to set healthy boundaries, but they will try to negotiate the situation to be a win-win for everyone involved, as opposed to railroading, playing games, or manipulating you.

Wouldn't it be nice to just be able to say what you want? "Can I have some of that?" That's the sort of question an assertive person asks. And an assertive person might answer, "No, you can't. I understand that your need is there, but I can't fulfill that for you right now. Maybe I can help you find someone who can."

I used to avoid people when I knew I'd have to say "no." I didn't want to disappoint them or look like the bad guy. I had family members who struggled with money, and sometimes they'd ask to borrow some. Instead of being assertive, I would complain about how poor I was or how hard my life was, or I would try to avoid the person altogether. I was trying to communicate, without actually saying it, that it was inappropriate for them to ask. This was because I didn't want to have to say "no". The scary thing is that my punking out on being assertive and "crying poor" became a self-fulfilling prophecy sometimes and I actually pissed away a lot of money and opportunities just so I could avoid disappointing people who asked me for stuff.

Now, after a lot of my own work on developing boundaries and increasing assertiveness, I interact with my family in a healthy way. They are allowed to ask for something, and I am allowed to say "no". I can speak to them honestly and openly.

Basically, being assertive means owning your shit. A lot of men have trouble apologizing for things, but giving a good apology is being assertive. It's owning up to your responsibility. Receiving a gift or a compliment graciously is assertive. It shows you are comfortable and confident. And giving a compliment when you don't expect anything in return is also an assertive statement.

The Danger of Being Unassertive

A study was done where people were told a secret and asked to keep it. A control group was not given a secret. Both groups were then asked to work out with physical weights. Those who had a secret to keep couldn't lift as much weight as those who did not. The secret was literally weighing them down!

This study used little, inconsequential secrets. Imagine the degree to which our secrets, anxieties, and unspoken truths are holding us back every day. Cumulative stress takes its toll.

If you made a commitment you can no longer honor – for instance, borrowing money from a friend that you're unable to pay back – an assertive response would be to be honest in this situation. As soon as you realize you cannot honor the commitment, communicate it to that person. By doing so, you are living a clean life. The stress of keeping it a secret will eat away at your strength.

The same thing happens in relationships. My rule of thumb is if I'm doing something with somebody and they rub me the wrong way or say something I don't like, I try to let it go if I can. If I can't let it go, though, I have to address it. I refuse to just bury it. Because I know that if I bury it, all sorts of stuff will go wrong later.

Burying anger and resentment causes the whole experience to harden into a brick of resentment until we don't even know why we're upset at this person any more. We just have this weird vibe when we're around that individual.

I tell people it's like using the bathroom. You flush the toilet every time you use it (for pretty obvious reasons). You should do the same thing when you're dealing with people. If there's shit in your life, flush it right now. Get rid of it so you don't have to carry it around with you or go through life dealing with the awful smell.

Chapter Nine

The Power of Purpose

> *"I finally figured out that it's easier to put on a pair of slippers than it is to try to carpet the whole world."*
>
> —STUART SMALLEY

The message behind the quote above (attributed to a *Saturday Night Live* character, believe it or not) is to give up on trying to make everything else in the world nice and cushy. Look after yourself first, and you will be all right.

I define "purpose" as having a sense of why you are here and why you are doing what you're doing. The honeybee is a good example of purpose. The honeybees gather nectar and pollen and create honey to feed their comrades, but the by-product of their mission is that they pollinate crops. Approximately one third of all the food Americans eat is directly or indirectly derived from honey bee pollination. [15]

I was at a workshop with one of my mentors, Blair Singer, author of *Sales Dogs* and *Little Voice Mastery*, who spoke about this concept. Bees don't intend to pollinate plants, they just do. They have amazing symbiotic relationships; in the process of gathering nectar, a bee gives back more to the flower. It transfers pollen grains from one flower to another, hence pollinating the flower for essential fertilization and reproduction to take place. Think of the amount of life on Earth that wouldn't exist if insects weren't out looking for nectar. The benefit to everyone else is the by-product of the bee's success, even though it's not their main purpose. Their main purpose is to get nectar for food and to feed the hive.

Having a sense of purpose, understanding what that is, and then pursuing and developing that is extremely important for your quality of life. It's about cultivating your own happiness and spreading it to others by extension – providing a benefit to everyone else as a by-product of your own fulfillment.

When you use The Me Factor process, you may realize, "Wow, I don't even know what works for me! I don't know what makes me happy. I don't know what I want."

You're not alone. Most people don't know where to start. That's why I have it laid out in a schematic. Ask yourself questions about each of the areas in your Me Factor Priority Schematic, and consider each of the Me Factors that make up the inner circle.

Start by asking the following questions:

- What is my purpose?
- What feels good to me?
- How much do I want in the bank?
- What do I want my physical health to look like?
- How much do I want to weigh?
- What kind of clothes do I want to wear?
- What kind of home do I want to live in?

It's necessary to ask these questions. It's not self-indulgence, and it's not frivolous. It's responsible. Asking these questions is a means to figuring out who you are and what you like.

Many people think they want what everybody else wants, but when they actually get it, they find that they never really wanted it at all. In fact, they don't really like it. They think they *should* like it, though, and they let that misguided feeling drag them down a desperate path. I've had clients who were in careers that other people envied. They were doing quite well, but they hated their jobs and felt guilty about hating them. In addition, hating the career they thought they *should* enjoy made them feel like they were being selfish or unappreciative, and that made them feel even more miserable.

It all comes back to the essential question I mentioned way back in Chapter One. *"Is this working for me?"*

It doesn't matter what other people think, and it doesn't matter what works for them. What works for *you*? When you start being true to that concept for yourself, not only do you learn more about yourself, but your self-esteem and your sense of personal power grow and your understanding of your own value increases.

Most people have the equation backward. They think that if they contribute a lot, it will make them happy. False. When you're happy, you contribute more. By looking after yourself, knowing who you are, and taking care of yourself, you will be a better you – a better husband, father, son, worker, and/or boss. You can't give from a place of emptiness; you can only give from fullness. The fuller you are, the more you have to offer.

It seems to me that most people have never heard the truth of finding what works for them. We don't teach this in schools, no one in the media is telling you this, you generally don't get this from church, and parents don't always have the knowledge or the time to teach it to their kids. You need to know that you have the right and responsibility to know who you are, what works for you, and what a big, full life looks like for you.

The bigger you live, the better you feel and the better you do. And the happier you are, the more you're able to contribute.

Keep in mind, your partner or your co-worker or your kids don't know what is going to work for you. They have a right to ask you, and you have a right to tell the truth. Everybody has that right, and that's how we get along with people. That's how we establish clean relationships, where things are open and straightforward.

Volunteering and Altruism

The central theme of The Me Factor is that you cannot give from a place of emptiness – at least not for long. It's unwise to give to the point of depletion. A lot of people, when they hear this, say, "If you did that, no one would volunteer or be altruistic."

Here is how I would respond. Recently, I was driving my daughter to school and a song came on the radio. It was pessimistic about life and the current state of the world. My daughter started to laugh. She said that the song reminded her of how so many of the people in her age group think about life. She said that they feel hopeless. I mentioned that part of the cause is that most people are distracted and lost because of technology and then they wonder why they feel their life has no joy or meaning.

I said that they need to step out of themselves and look at how they can make a difference in someone else's life or contribute to the world in some way. She said that they all feel like they can't make a difference because of the system having too much negative inertia. I helped her understand that anyone can make a difference, maybe not in changing the whole world by themselves, but to the people they serve. The idea is to get small in your thinking. You don't need permission to start your own campaign to pick up litter in your community or show kindness to service people or adopt an underprivileged school (or class or student) and take supplies to them.

Any of these activities changes your experience of yourself and your life. And it doesn't necessarily take a bunch of money or time. Just do what you can out of your joy and desire to help and see how the energy flows back into your life.

Finding a cause you can believe in and invest yourself in adds depth, meaning and a sense of purpose to life. When you don't have a well to dip into that is bigger than just feeding your own desires, the desires begin to lose their value. When you give to something or someone outside yourself it makes everything else you have and do feel several times more enjoyable and fulfilling. I have several wealthy clients who routinely donate their time and/or money to things like community leagues, amateur sports, schools/universities, homeless shelters, Habitat for Humanity, and food banks. They get excited, both about providing money, time, and energy and their *ability* to do these things. They are giving from their overflow. They feel so blessed and fortunate to be living the life they've created for themselves that they want to share that with as many people as they can.

Many people are altruistic or volunteer because of their religious tenets or because they feel it's their duty. We all want to be good people. The source of this is an outside force or influence that causes us to volunteer and/or be altruistic. This is not the best way to approach altruism.

Anybody who has spent time in the nonprofit sector has likely come across a miserable-looking, pissed-off, burned-out volunteer or employee. They might feel it's their duty to be there, but they certainly don't *want* to be there. They're angry, frustrated, resentful, and no fun to be around.

Humans can feel other people's energy and automatically absorb their moods. We might not always recognize it or be able to put words to it, but we definitely feel it; it's an innate part of our nervous system and our subconscious. Just by being in the presence of those pissed-off volunteers, you can feel your own energy being sucked away. Imagine what it's like for the people receiving these services to have that type of negative energy around them, or to feel guilty or "less than" because the people providing services they need are so angry all the time.

Acting according to a sense of duty doesn't allow you to feel the advantage of what you're doing. It may feel good in the moment to serve lunch at a homeless shelter, but you do not get the full benefit of giving out joy if you don't really want to be there in the first place. The people who are being served often don't receive the full benefit of having a joyful person working with them. It's not sustainable to give from guilt or obligation or fear or any of these other external motivators.

It's far better to give from joy.

The aim of The Me Factor System is to help you take responsibility for your life. If you understand that it's your right and responsibility to feel good, to fill yourself up, to look after your own needs first, then you can give from a place of abundance. You give because you can't contain yourself any more. You give from joy. That is an entirely different experience for you as you give, and a very different experience for the person receiving the gift.

The idea is not to get rid of volunteering. The idea is to take a break from giving for the wrong reasons. Take care of yourself first so it can lead you organically to wanting to contribute.

If you were to take a hiatus from volunteering to work on yourself – to make sure you are getting sufficient sleep, doing things you enjoy, eating well, exercising, hanging out with good people, fulfilling your emotional, physical, spiritual, intellectual, and financial needs – it's very likely that you would have an overwhelming need to share from your bounty with others. You would discover the right outlet to fulfill that feeling. You would also do it in a paced, measured way so you don't burn out from doing too much, which can cause you to start resenting the very people and organizations you are trying to help.

Imagine what it would be like if all the pissed-off volunteers took the time first to look after themselves. Let's say they followed The Me Factor System and started to look after their own needs in a responsible way. All of a sudden, when they show up to work they're feeling happy. There's a different energy being provided to the people they are serving. It really would make a difference.

The movie *The Pursuit of Happyness*, starring Will Smith, is inspired by the true story of Chris Gardner, a salesman struggling to make ends meet and build a future for himself and his son. He and his son become homeless and have to sleep in the subway bathroom when there is no room in the shelter. Chris is determined to become a stockbroker, and the movie follows his journey working an internship to get his qualifications. He has no money in the meantime and has to support his son.

When the movie came out, Chris Gardner went on *Oprah* to talk about his experiences. One of the things that really struck me was that he said he used to go to Glide Memorial Church in San Francisco, and one of the things that kept him going was the absolute joy and happiness the volunteers had when they saw him. He and his son felt truly welcome at this mission. That little bit of energy, that smile, that eye contact, that joy shown by the people volunteering at Glide made all the difference for Chris and helped him have the faith to keep going, look after his son, and achieve his goals. Chris was able to break through. Think about how that energy keeps going. Chris now provides for his son, his employees, the tax base, businesses and services he uses, and contributes to his community. The energy of giving from a place of joy has had positive practical and economic consequences.

That's what happens when you put yourself first. You have genuine, organic joy from your bones. Not just paste-on-a-smile or pretend-to-be-polite joy. When it comes to altruism, giving for the sake of giving is best when it comes from a place of overabundance. You feel it and want to share it.

I don't believe in the concept of pure altruism. It's more like enlightened self-interest. The more you give from pure joy, the better you feel. You're getting something from the act. You're getting something from giving because you enjoy it!

If you don't enjoy it and you're giving for another reason, you're still getting something. You get to "sacrifice". You get to feel like a good person. You get to tell people that you volunteered. Or maybe you feel you get saved from hell.

Nobody gives purely because other people need it, without getting anything from it. It's more intellectually and spiritually honest to recognize you're getting something from this.

When I volunteer at the homeless shelter or work with kids, coach hockey or basketball, or give a free session or talk, I'm contributing to a better culture, to helping other people find a better way. I get a sense of contribution, I get appreciation from the people I'm serving and I get the sense of satisfaction knowing I am doing something larger than myself. We're creating a better society. We're creating a better world by teaching kids skills so they can be happier.

If we can get to a point where we are all doing this from a place of joy, it will reduce crime. It will reduce poverty and violence, and that benefits us all. That's what I mean when I say altruism is enlightened self-interest; we are all benefiting from the good that we do in the world.

Everything comes full circle. You get what you give. The bigger your investment, the more you get back. I'm certainly not against volunteering, but I am against volunteering for external reasons. It's far better to take some time, regroup, fill your cup first, and then volunteer when you overflow with joy and abundance.

If you are burned out and depleted, take a hiatus. When you do come back, pace yourself. Work in conjunction with the law of diminishing returns to prevent burnout. You are giving quality. You're also experiencing your highest performance, and that spreads beyond volunteer activity, reaching out into your whole life.

Your Twofold Purpose

If you've never taken the time to think about your purpose, it can seem like a lot of work to figure it out. Don't think of it as something you have to nail down in order to be complete. You've lived this long already, so you're all right, right where you are. You've made it. You're okay!

Instead, think of this as an adventure. Your mission is to explore, figure things out, and learn. Think of it as something you *get* to do. You get to enjoy and learn more about yourself day by day, little by little.

There are two distinct elements of your purpose as a man in this world, which I'll discuss in the following pages. To discover yours, I recommend trying as many new activities as you can to see what ignites you. You might find that some of the things that used to work for you don't work any more, or what you thought would work probably never did in the first place. Take your time and know that discovering your purpose is an adventure.

This an expedition! You're climbing the Andes Mountains. You're blazing a trail through the heart of the wilderness. Get out and enjoy it.

My belief is that we all have two purposes. The first is something we all share, and the second is something particular to each of us.

Purpose #1: Happiness

My psychologist likes to say, "It's a sad dog who can't wag his own tail." It's a statement that speaks to our first purpose in life.

Purpose #1 is to be happy – end of story. There's no other reason for us to be here. It's not about obligation; it's not about leaving a mark. It doesn't matter if anybody remembers you or not, as long as you're happy. Figure out what makes you happy without changing other people. Wag your damn tail!

Ask yourself:

- What makes me happy with my partner?
- What makes me happy being a parent?
- What makes me happy in my sense of purpose and my sense of spirituality?
- What fills me up?

We may not always know the answers in the abstract sense, but if you try some new things, you will make some life-changing discoveries.

For instance, let's say you want to try mountain climbing. You might realize it's hard, but you love it! On the other hand, your response might be, "This really sucks, and I don't like it." So it is not going to be on your list any more. It's as simple as that. This is a journey to find out what feels right for you. As with your internal tuning fork, you will *know*, because it will resonate with you. It will feel right.

Don't worry about making mistakes in the process. This idea of not making mistakes – perfectionism – is a killer of happiness. We *learn* by making mistakes.

Here's how it should work: Do something. It works or it doesn't work. You record the result. You make better decisions moving forward based on that information. That's life.

A few years ago, I decided to buy a car. My psychologist at the time suggested I test-drive a number of different cars. He even suggested I go out of my way to test-drive cars I really didn't think I would like. He reminded me that it was not just important to know what I liked – to have the feeling of what was right for me – but also to know what it feels like when I *don't* like something. Trying new things is how we know. I took his advice and was surprised by the results. Identifying cars that definitely did not work for me went a long way toward identifying the one that did.

Trying new things is how you figure out who you are. You can use your Me Factor Priority Schematic to create a list of what makes you happy in different areas, starting with your Me Factors. Once you have that exercise done, you can turn it into your ideal life. Some people put it on their vision boards; others hold the vision as their aspirational idea of what they want to work toward.

What matters is this: Are you happy? Happiness informs your second purpose.

Purpose #2: Your Unique Mission

I often hear people voice the belief that you must find your unique purpose and pursue it or express it in order to be happy. I say it's the other way around.

When you know that happiness comes first and you do what makes you happy, your unique purpose is naturally expressed. For me, I love helping people grow. That is my mission. When I am happy and doing what I love, my purpose helps other people.

Some people love building beautiful furniture, caring for children, healing the sick, making music, or writing books. By doing what makes you happy, you are fulfilling your second purpose, which is helping other people, however that may be.

I used to think I should be a doctor or a minister because they help people. But neither of those callings, noble as they may be, would have been true to who I am. It might have impressed other people, but it wouldn't have been fulfilling to me.

In Andre Agassi's autobiography, *Open*, he shares that he did not like tennis. Imagine that! One of the greatest tennis players of all time didn't even like the game! But because he was good at it, people made him their own little personal economy. Soon, he was supporting a lot of people with his talent. But he didn't enjoy what he did. Because of that, he said he really didn't go as far as he could have.

Agassi was unhappy, had all sorts of issues with drugs and alcohol abuse, suffered through failed relationships, and went through some real turmoil in his personal life. He made it pretty far, considering he disliked what he did. He won the Grand Slam eight times and a gold medal at the Olympics in 1996. Consider how much further he could have gone if he had gotten satisfaction and enjoyment out of what he did and enjoyed his life outside of work?

Unfortunately, this happens to men all the time. They are good at something or have been told they are supposed to do something – maybe it's expected of them or it's the family tradition – so that's what they choose to do. But it's not true to who they are, and they suffer for it. They might still be successful at it even if they're unhappy, but they'll never be as fulfilled as they would have been if they were in alignment with their internal sense of who they are.

It's important for you to be mindful of what makes you happy and to investigate what these things are. Ask yourself:

- What kinds of things make me happy?
- Where do I find my joy?
- What creates that feeling of flow or being "in the zone" in my life?

It should be freeing to realize that Purpose #2 is essentially an extension of Purpose #1, and both are about being happy. Happiness is your purpose! And when you are living on purpose instead of doing things out of obligation, you have more energy. You are full rather than depleted. This is how you know you're on your correct path.

Chapter Ten

Another look at the Priorities Schematic

The Me Factor System works from the inside out. That means you always have to consider the deeper internal factors, the "ME", before looking at the outer ones. You need to feed and protect the innermost parts of your Priority Schematic first.

Boundaries and protection are really important. Trust me, nothing can stress you out like a bad relationship with your partner and kids. You can't enjoy all the success you've worked so hard to achieve because of the fights – and you eventually end up giving most of your money away to the divorce lawyers. Your college education fund becomes a legal defense fund because your poor relationship with your kids causes them to struggle and have trouble with the law.

On the other hand, when you follow the system all these priorities get fed and are in balance. The beauty of following this system is that once you start, the energy you pour in comes back to you with interest. You actually end up with more energy than you put in! But you have to stick with it.

You also have to protect the other priorities in your schematic from things and people on the outside. Only things that feed everything on the inside are allowed through your boundaries. In addition, the extra energy you now have (from not being depleted) flows from the center, making you better at the Priorities as you move out from the "ME" circle – being a better partner, parent, friend, family member, and employee.

As you move out from the center the next priority you come to is "Partner". Here are some thoughts on how to help feed this next important dimension.

Be a Good Husband

Love, validate, accept, and support. Those are the key ingredients to a healthy marriage.

Men are fixers. When we see something that looks broken, we try to fix it. But when your partner is having a hard time, you need to *understand* that they're having a hard time. When they're feeling insecure, the mistake is thinking it's your job to make them feel secure. You can't! It's impossible. What they need is for you to *understand* that they're feeling insecure, validate how they feel and know that it is real for them. Even if you don't agree with their thoughts on the matter, even if you think it's trivial - even if you don't think it's real - it is real for them in this moment.

Most men, when presented with a problem, assume that it's their responsibility to find a solution. I've found that in all relationships, interactions basically come down to *agreements* versus *assumptions*. My advice: make agreements, don't make assumptions.

Trying to fix your partner means you're trying to *change* your partner, and the message they receive is that they're not good enough. You may think you're helping, but you are actually hurting them. Don't *assume* they need your help. *Agree* that their feelings are real, valid, and important to you. By listening, accepting, and understanding how your spouse feels – by not freaking out or trying to "fix" them - you can build their self-esteem. It helps them to know that they can be themselves. They can fall apart and be a hot mess for now if they need to, and it's okay because they know *My husband loves me.* And remember that in any relationship the roles will be reversed at some point in the future.

You also need to present a unified front with your spouse in public, with friends and family, and especially with your kids. Not backing them up, rolling your eyes, or making jokes at their expense is a sure way to erode your relationship. Your job is to build them up in other people's eyes – not tear them down. If there are any issues, deal with them at home. Don't complain to your buddies about them and definitely don't complain to other people within your "attraction gender" (i.e. other women, like your buddies' wives). I've seen way too many affairs start that way and it's a shit show for everyone involved. Deal directly with your partner, and leave the complaining for your journal and the psychologist you are working with.

The Wall of China

When it comes to boundaries, you may have noticed in your Priority Schematic that the one around "Kids", Partner" and "Me" is much thicker than the others. That's because this isn't just a double fence – this one is the Wall of China! You really need to protect this "sacred circle".

If you're a parent, you have the right and a responsibility to *only* let in people, ideas, advice, and activities that work for everyone inside that circle. Well-meaning people (like grandparents and other family and friends) can cause real damage to your relationship with your partner and your kids if that boundary isn't strong. They don't always understand the best way to help. They need to know where the lines are and who calls the shots. They should play a supporting role, not the main one, and back you guys up as the parents. That means supporting your rules and not questioning you or making "suggestions" in front of the kids.

If you think the women in your life could benefit from something like this, too, go to TheMeFactor.me and click "The She Factor" for a free checklist just for her.

Parenting

Kids learn what they live. This means that you, as a kid, also learned what was "normal" by seeing what was around you. It's going to be easy for you and your partner to pass all the good, the bad *and* the ugly on to your kids if you're not paying attention. This is a good place to use the question: "Is this working for me?" You can then become aware that what you thought of as "normal" may actually be pretty harmful, and then deliberately choose something more positive to pass on to your kids.

One of the big reasons I became a psychologist was that I grew up in a pretty dysfunctional family. I learned firsthand what happens when parents don't have their own shit together and how that affects the kids. I wanted to learn about that in the hopes of helping others, and I also wanted to avoid that path for my kids.

It starts by knowing who you are. Take care of your own needs, health and well-being first. If you don't, you will suck what you need out of everybody around you, your partner, and especially your children.

Kids have not been on Earth long enough to have developed healthy boundaries, so they are easy victims. They take on everything! They think everything is their fault or that they are the reason everything happens. It goes directly to their sense of self and affects their self-esteem and their identity.

The more you love yourself, take care of yourself, and take responsibility for your own needs, the healthier your kids will be. The healthier your kids are, the happier they are, and the more successful they will be in their personal lives and future careers.

It's incredibly important that the adults in the home *be* the adults in the home. The adults are in charge, not the kids.

Parenting trends come in waves. The 1950s were known for restrictive parenting, a demanding, punishment-heavy style where parents were over-controlling and kids followed directions with little or no explanation or feedback. By the late 90s, we saw a wave of helicopter parents, those who took an overprotective or excessive interest in their children. Then we saw a wave of parents who wanted to be friends with their kids and allow them to have the freedom to make their own choices.

The style I disagree with most is the last option, as children don't have enough knowledge to make certain choices. Child-centric parenting simply doesn't work. Free-range parenting doesn't work. The household is not a democracy. It's a benevolent dictatorship. The adults are the dictators; the kids are the subjects. You do everything in their best interests and you take their wants and needs and desires into account, but you don't defer to their judgment – because they're kids! You can ask them for their opinions, but it has to be clear that the final decision rests with the parent. If you give them the opportunity to choose, it has to be clear that you are *giving* them that opportunity, as opposed to it being their right. They get to decide because you gave them permission, not because they have the right to make the decision.

What Kind of Dad Are You?

The old archetype for Dad was the guy who shows up and spanks you when you're bad. He'll carve the turkey on Thanksgiving, but there's not a lot of emotional closeness.

We've seen what happens to children who grew up with cold, distant fathers, and it's not good. It leads to higher instances of drug abuse, alcoholism, depression, and anxiety, and that's just for starters. Being able to connect with your kids and show vulnerability – that is a higher definition of strength.

Despite what I said about kids not having the right to make decisions, as parents, it's up to us to help our kids learn to be good decision-makers. The parents set the boundaries. It's like a little box. The kids have freedom, as long as they stay within the box. When they're little, you give them choices:

"Do you want the red socks or the blue socks?"

"I want to wear sandals!"

"Nope, that's not the choice. Blue socks or red socks. You get to choose that. And you don't get to choose what color pants you wear...or whether you wear pants."

You define the choices for them.

The consequences for straying outside the box should be consistent. They should reflect reality and be equivalent to the severity of the violation without being unrealistic. If your kid is five minutes late for curfew, they shouldn't be grounded for two months. The consequences should never be that extreme. The reward for staying in the box is peace and happiness, a "good job" and maybe an allowance or some other privilege.

As they get older, the box gets bigger, and they have more freedom within it. Your job as the adult, the parent, is to define the box. It should be reasonable and things should reflect how the real world works. It shouldn't vary based on what mood you're in. It shouldn't vary based on, "Well, Mom lets us get away with this, but Dad is strict," or *vice versa*. It has to be consistent over time and consistent between caregivers.

Your kids' job, by the way, is to try to get out of the box you put there. This is how they learn to become individuals. It's how they build their self-esteem and identity. It's also why, when they reach adolescence, they get weird haircuts and listen to weird music and wear weird clothes. It's how they show their individuality. Adolescents are eager to prove they are not just miniature versions of their parents.

Don't take it personally when your kids try to get out of the box. After all, you did the same thing when you were a kid. Your kids are supposed to do that, and it's an important part of development. Your job is still to maintain the box and maintain those boundaries.

As your kids get older and the box gets bigger, ideally they will internalize those limits and own the structures you've laid down. If they don't, then society has its own box for them, and it's made of solid walls, steel bars, and has armed guards.

Your House: A Microcosm of Reality

I see the home as a little microcosm of reality. When we go out into the real world, people don't do things for us. No one is anticipating my needs and doing everything so I don't have to. I do it myself. So, what do you think you might be subtly communicating to your children when you do everything for them at home?

The rules of the house need to reflect the rules of society. In other words, what happens in the house has to match what happens in the real world. If you mouth off to your boss, you'll get fired. If your children mouth off to their parents, there needs to be a similar consequence. If they can mouth off without consequences, you're not doing your job to train them to live a successful life.

Let's say I'm renting an apartment and I throw my garbage out in the hall. Will I be able to stay in that apartment for very long? No! It's the same with your kids; if they don't clean their room or are always leaving their belongings in the common areas, and the parents do not address this behavior, then the parents aren't teaching the child to be a successful member of society.

Present a Unified Front

Notice, in the Me Factor Priority Schematic, that there is a boundary between the Partner/Spouse section and the Children section. There's a good reason I don't just lump these two categories into a general "Immediate Family" section. It's because you and your partner come first. You have to be together because kids will break you apart if you let them.

Parents must always remember to work together. You can't undermine each other, and there can't be a good cop/bad cop situation – or bad cop/worse cop. All communication between parents and children must be in "we" terms. "*We* feel this way. *We* think this is the best approach. We agree."

It doesn't matter who is speaking. The adult doing the speaking speaks for all the adults. You have to back each other up!

If parents disagree about a boundary or decision, they must remove the discussion from the kids. Sit down in private and work it out. The kids should not be privy to this conversation. Reaching a consensus is best, but you might have to settle for a solution you can both live with. While a compromise is not always ideal, it's better than two conflicting and inconsistent messages. You have to be together on this.

Consistency is better than perfection. It is better to have three rules that you enforce consistently and that everybody can adhere to than to have twenty rules you only sometimes enforce. Discuss these things. If you're not on the same page, it will not work.

Just to be clear. Disagreements in general aren't the problem. If you disagree with one another in front of the kids it should be done in a respectful way – and the kids should also be able to witness (or at least be aware of) the resolution of the disagreement. This is healthy modeling of how to disagree agreeably and how to come to terms after. It also reassures the kids that a disagreement is not the end of the relationship. The partner and family relationships are based on a much stronger foundation of love and understanding – so are not threatened by a momentary difference of opinion. However, if it's a disagreement *about* the kids, that has to happen away from their eyes and ears.

If, say, you come home from work to find your partner grounding your teenager for the next thirty years, don't intervene. Let the scene play out. Even if it seems crazy, let it play out. When he or she calms down, take them aside and say, "You know, honey, if they're grounded for thirty years, we're grounded for thirty years, too, because we have to be home to make sure *they're* home. Maybe we can find a different solution that might be more reasonable. Maybe they're grounded for the weekend. What do you think?" Once you're in agreement, the parent who did the grounding should be the one to go back and fix it. Saying something like "*We* discussed this and here is the new deal…"

Sometimes, the opposite happens, where there's no consequence given and the other parent comes in crying for justice, saying things like, "Are you kidding me? You can't let them get away with that! Bring the hammer down!" The person who doled out the punishment is still the one who reports the new plan. In this case, they would go back to the child and say, "I'm sorry. I was not doing my job as a parent. We talked about it. Here's what the consequence is going to be."

In neither situation, under any circumstances, should you say, "Well, your Mom thinks I'm too slack, so here's what we have to do now," or, "Mom thinks I was too hard on you." You have to present a united front at all times.

Ultimately, our role as parents is to raise happy, healthy, productive members of society. The first step is to keep our children safe. We have to provide shelter and food. But we also have to provide training for them so they know how to "do life." Our job is to create a little microcosm of how the world works, in our homes, so they learn to understand the rules by living them.

If you've signed up to be a parent, do your work. If you signed up to be half of a couple, do your work. It's not okay to abdicate responsibility. That's not fair to the other person in the relationship, and it's definitely not fair to the kids. They need healthy, engaged parents.

Again, this is why "Me" is at the center. *You* have to do your work. Talk to a therapist. If you're in a relationship, the two of you should talk to a therapist together. Do your own personal work to become more assertive by finding a book on the topic or taking an assertiveness training course. Do what you need to do because it's not fair to let your partner handle everything. No good cop/bad cop. Get on the same page and stay there.

With blended families becoming more common, here are a few special considerations:

1. Your kids have feelings too. They can't just be along for the ride as you look for a new relationship. Take the time to get to know the other person and make sure its going somewhere before introducing the kids to him or her. You don't want a parade of losses in your kid's life or they will just stop getting attached in the first place.
2. The new adult in the kid's life doesn't have the same track record as the biological parent. So the bio parent has to be the point person and the new adult the back-up parent. The new person can't replace the parent who is gone or died.

3. Go slow with establishing the new adult as an authority figure. They need to just support you. The new partner should say things like, "We'll have to discuss that with your dad before we decide".
4. In some cases, the kids will be in the closer circle than the new girlfriend/boyfriend until the relationship is solid and going places. You can ask how the kids feel and take all this into consideration, but you should **never** leave the decision of whom you date up to your kids. That's way too much power and pressure for someone who is young.
5. You and your new partner must do everything possible from a parenting perspective to support the other biological parent (and their new relationship). The ideal situation is to have consistent rules in both homes, if possible. If that is not possible, support the other parent's household rules and structure as long as they are healthy. This is better for the kids. The worst-case scenario is when one parent is criticizing the other. Intuitively, children understand that they are half of each of you. When one parent is "bad", then they feel they are "bad" as well. It is detrimental for their self-esteem and sense of identity and is confusing in terms of what is expected of them.

For additional support with your relationships or parenting, go to TheMeFactor.me and sign up for my FREE Master Class and ask me your burning questions on these topics.

Chapter Eleven

The Decision Matrix and Implementing the Me Factor System

When you set up your Me Factor System correctly and place your priorities in the right order, even when you pour massive amounts of energy into the system, you get more back. This chapter is about making critical life decisions and a "how-to" for implementing your Me Factor System.

The Decision Matrix

The Decision Matrix is the next step in the Me Factor System once you've filled out your Owner's Manual. It's a tool I developed to help my students (and myself) make decisions taking into account all the Me Factors and the Priorities in your Schematic.

ME FACTOR DECISION MATRIX

FACTORS	DECISIONS							
Physical								
Emotional								
Intellectual								
Spiritual								
Financial								
Social								
Purpose								
Subtotal (Internal) Me								
Partner								
Kids								
Extended Family + Friends								
Work								
Subtotal (External) Everyone Else								
Grand Total								

©Copyright 2018 Dr. Ganz Ferrance

Use the tools to help you get what the HELL you want. Download free copies of this and all my graphics at TheMeFactor.me

1. Put the choices at the top of each column under "decisions". It is best to calculate for one decision at a time

2. Ask: **What is the net effect of this choice on my well-being or my "Fuel Tank" for this factor?**
   i. Use a scale of -10 to +10.
   ii. Negative numbers indicate a cost or energy leak.
   iii. Positive numbers indicate a benefit or energy deposit.
   iv. Zero indicates no effect on that area.

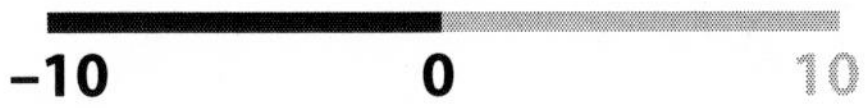

3. Evaluate the net energy effect on all seven Me Factors. This is your "Me" subtotal. This is how the decision will affect you – not counting everyone and everything else in your Me Factor Priority Schematic.
4. What is the net effect of this choice for the Partner, Kids, Extended Family and Friends, and Work dimensions?
5. Add the scores for Partner, Kids, Extended Family and Friends, and Work dimensions. This becomes your sub-total (external).
6. Add the two sub totals (Me/internal and external) to get your grand total for that choice/column.
7. Repeat steps 1 through 6 for each alternative choice.

Based on the scores, which choice is best for you at this time? (You have a potential high score of 110 and low score of -110)

Other Considerations:

- Is there a need to prioritize any of these factors more highly right now?
- What are the long AND short-term effects on these factors for each scenario?
- Just because a scenario comes out higher than another doesn't mean you have to choose that one. You just have a clearer idea about what the cost/benefit of each choice

will be. You can choose a lower value scenario if there are other factors that weigh more heavily (like partner, kids, or finances). But you now have a way of looking at how to minimize the negative effects and/or create more positive effects to counter-balance the cost. An example is continuing to stay in a location you hate because the financial loss from selling your home would be too high. You may take more frequent vacations and look for positive things in your location to make staying more palatable.

The Decision Matrix in Action

Here's how this works: In Chapter Three, I told you about two men who attended a Me Factor workshop and used this system. The first guy, Richard, needed to decide if he should move out of his current situation with his roommate and find his own place to live. When he looked at staying put, he found the following for each factor:

FACTORS	DECISIONS	SCORE
Physical	He wasn't sleeping well and didn't feel comfortable in his own place.	-5
Emotional	He was pissed off all the time and didn't like the negativity his roommate constantly spewed.	-8
Intellectual	Because of the negative daily experience he found that he was distracted and couldn't focus the way he should.	-5
Spiritual	Richard was so distracted and influenced by the negative environment that he was starting to becoming negative himself and neglecting this dimension (he also never thought of this dimension before the workshop).	-2

FACTORS	DECISIONS	SCORE
Financial	Living with his roommate was a smokin' deal financially. He was able to save a ton of money and live cheaply.	+9
Social:	Because he felt uncomfortable at home he didn't have friends over much – but did spend time out of the house with his friends.	-2
Purpose	This was a non-factor in this decision.	0

Richard's "ME" subtotal was for staying was -31

External Factors:

Partner	He wasn't married and wasn't currently in a relationship or looking.	0
Kids	No children	0
Extend-ed Family and friends	He didn't have family members over much because of tension with the roommate.	-2
Work	His place was an easy commute to his job.	+3

Richard's "Everything else" subtotal was +1.

His grand total was -30. It was costing him energy just to stay put in his current living situation.

Now let's look at the "move out" option:

FACTORS	DECISIONS	SCORE
Physical	He felt that having his own space and being comfortable would help him sleep better and even start to work out at home.	+6
Emotional	Richard knew that being in a more positive (or even neutral) environment would do wonders for his emotional health.	+9

FACTORS	DECISIONS	SCORE
Intellectual	He felt he would be much sharper if he were happier – a pretty good assumption.	+4
Spiritual	Once he understood about this dimension he figured that if he had his own space he could invest in this factor more.	+6
Financial	Unfortunately, Richard currently didn't have the money it would take to get the kind of place he wanted. He would also have to carry the rent all by himself.	-4
Social:	He knew he would entertain more in his own place.	+6
Purpose	This was a non-factor in this decision.	0

So Richard's Internal "Me" subtotal was +27.

External Factors:

Partner	Same as above, not a factor	0
Kids	Same as above, not a factor.	0
Extend-ed Family and friends	He felt these relationships would be better.	+5
Work	Richard would look for a place close to work but he felt that even if he had to travel a bit more, his work would be better if he was happier – another good assumption.	+3

His External subtotal was +8.

Richard had a Grand total of +34. This meant that the choice to move was even more positive than choosing to stay was negative. Staying was costing him energy while it would definitely feed him to move.

Richard chose to stay while he got his finances together and eventually got his own place. He talked to me later and said that he was way healthier and happier now. He used this information to put more focus on things that fed him so he could stay in the financially beneficial situation while he got his act together. He also shared that he had felt unbalanced the whole time he was with his roommate but could never really understand why. This system gave him a framework to understand how he was feeling and why. It made perfect sense to him once he went through this exercise.

Example 2: Stay or Leave A Job

The other example from Chapter three was Charles, who didn't like his job but was nervous about jumping ship. Here's how his decision matrix looked.

Decision: To stay at current job:

FACTORS	DECISIONS	SCORE
Physical	He was super overworked and stressed out by his boss. He wasn't sleeping and had high blood pressure. His doctor was concerned.	-9
Emotional	Charles was on antidepressants and was always pissed off and on edge.	-10
Intellectual	All this stress took a toll on his mental sharpness and intellectual functioning.	-8
Spiritual	He was being negative and stopped feeding himself in this area.	-3
Financial	This job had always paid well and he had a good reputation with the company because he had been there a long time. But he was also quite marketable in his field.	+2

FACTORS	DECISIONS	SCORE
Social:	Charles worked so hard that he was too exhausted to have a social life.	-8
Purpose	He had originally loved this job as it fit his idea of his purpose. But over time the job and the culture changed and Charles also evolved. It no longer fed him in this area. In fact, it was actually counter to how he wanted to live.	-8

Charles' "ME" subtotal was -44.

External Factors:

Partner	His negative mood as well as the lack of time and energy really hurt his relationship with his wife.	-6
Kids	These same issues caused problems in his relationship with his kids, too.	-7
Extended Family and friends	Same deal here.	-6
Work	Charles found that because the job no longer worked in so many areas that his quality and productivity were starting to slip. Of course, this just stressed him out more.	-2

His External subtotal was -21. And his Grand total -65. He was being drained by his job.

When he looked at the new opportunity he had (going to the interview that afternoon) it came out like this:

Decision: New job

FACTORS	DECISIONS	SCORE
Physical	He knew he would feel better with less stress and a more balanced work schedule.	+3

FACTORS	DECISIONS	SCORE
Emotional	He really liked the company culture and their emphasis on "work/life balance." Just doing the research on the job gave him an emotional lift.	+8
Intellectual	He figured if he were happier and getting more sleep he would be sharper. This job also challenged him intellectually.	+5
Spiritual	Because of the better schedule and more reasonable job demands, Charles felt he would have the energy to invest in his spiritual life again.	+3
Financial	This job paid about the same as the other one.	+2
Social:	More time, energy and a better attitude meant he would probably want to reach out to friends more (and he wouldn't scare them away).	+5
Purpose	This was a big one for Charles. This company had the values and culture that fit his new approach to life and contribution.	He gave this a +9

His Internal subtotal for the new job was +23.

External Factors:

Partner	His wife was totally on board with the switch and Charles could see how more time and a better attitude would build a better relationship with her.	+8
Kids	Same with his kids.	+8
Extended Family and friends	Charles realized that he had actually been a bit MIA with his extended family and that this new job would give him time and energy to reconnect with them.	+5
Work	He was excited about work again. This new energy could translate into better productivity and possibly advancement.	+8

For the new job Charles had an external subtotal of +29. His Grand total was +52. That's a 117-point swing. He was losing energy (-65) by staying and had a potential of gaining in a huge way if he switched jobs. Once he saw this, the decision became a no-brainer for him. His fear and concern evaporated and he took the new job that very afternoon.

Try this powerful tool for yourself and let me know how it worked for you. Go to TheMeFactor.me and drop me a line in the comments section.

Dr. Ganz's Ten-Point Scale

I have a Ten-Point Scale I teach in my classes. I personally use it to make sure I'm on the right track.

I developed this scale because I have struggled with depression in the past and have even been on medication a couple of times. This is one of the things I have been talking to my psychologist about. To be clear, I am a practicing psychologist, and I see a psychologist regularly. In fact, I've been talking to a psychologist for the last twenty-seven years; I wouldn't sell the product if I didn't use it myself.

I use the Ten-Point Scale to determine when I need a boost in a specific area of my life, because if I get too low in any given category, it is hard to pull up again. This is a quick and dirty way of seeing where I am if I don't have the time to do a full personal diagnostic.

A rating of ten means I'm the happiest I've ever been, and one would mean I need to be hospitalized. I ask myself, "How am I doing? What's my number today?" If I'm a seven or above, I'm okay. I like to be an eight or nine, and obviously, ten would be great. But if I get to a seven or below, I look at the list of activities on my Me Factor Owner's Manual (or check out the Emergency Plan on Page 183) and do something on my list some time that week because I don't want to slide below a seven.

If I find I'm at a six, I have to do something today, and if I find that I'm at a five, I have to do something *right now*. Once I get below a five, everything suffers. It takes more energy to do the things I normally enjoy.

If you're at a five or below, it also might take more energy to start this process. Sometimes, just learning the process can help you get through – understanding that even though you feel like crap, you can still do what usually helps you because there will probably be some good that comes of it at the end. Sometimes, that alone gives you enough motivation.

For example, when I was taking karate classes, sometimes I would reach a five or even a four on my Ten-Point Scale. I wouldn't want to go to karate, and this is something I have always enjoyed. I could easily talk myself out of going to the dojo even though I knew full well that if I went, I would feel better. I knew it was something I wanted to do, but the energy to do it just wasn't there.

Sometimes, I'd even try to force myself. I'd go put on my outfit and drive to the dojo. I'd sit in the parking lot and look at the building. And then I'd drive home because I just didn't have the energy to go inside. But I soon learned that if I did go in, I would have a good workout, feel great, and actually bring my mood up by a number or two.

These days, I try a different tactic. I don't allow myself to get to the point where I have to force myself to do anything. For me, that means I don't let myself drop below a five or a six.

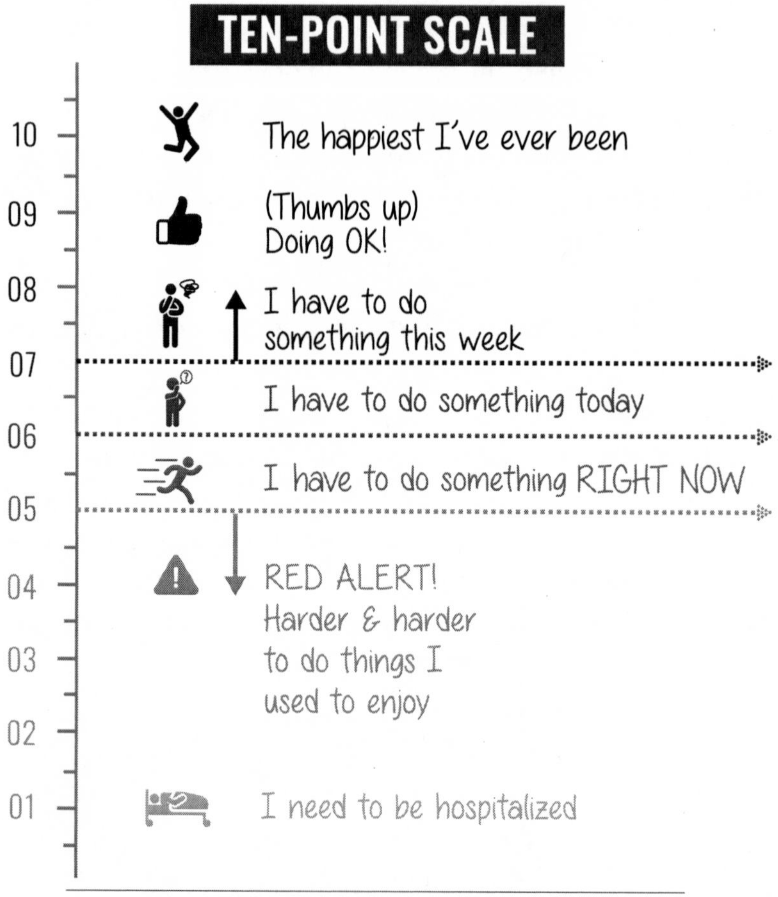
TEN-POINT SCALE
10
The happiest I've ever been
09
(Thumbs up)
Doing OK!
08
I have to do
something this week
07
I have to do something today
06
I have to do something RIGHT NOW
05
04
RED ALERT!
Harder & harder
to do things I
used to enjoy
03
02
01
I need to be hospitalized

1. **Ask Yourself:**
   How am I doing?
2. **Evaluate Yourself:**
   Where do you fall between 1-10?
3. **Take Action:**
   Schedule something based on your score.

©Copyright 2018 Dr. Ganz Ferrance

Use the tools to help you get what the HELL you want. Download free copies of this and all my graphics at TheMeFactor.me

Have an Emergency Plan

I know that when I hit a five, it's time to just cancel my day and go see a movie. As you start filling out the Me Factor Owner's Manual, you will come up with your own emergency plan. It's like the procedure binder/envelope you see in those action movies. Some crisis comes up and the guy in the bunker rips open the emergency envelope and starts following the steps.

I have a list of five to ten things that I know I can do that will pull me out of a nosedive and help me feel better. If I am at a seven, I know I have to do one of the following: ride my bike, play basketball, call a friend, or leave town and spend time outside/in nature.

I have my contingency plan. I know my instructions. I have the steps written down, and I know what to do. In fact, I've been following them long enough that they're in my head now. I know that I can do any one of these things, or the other activities listed on my Me Factor Owner's Manual, to start to feel better.

Dr. Ganz's Emergency Plan

Here are some of the things I use for my personal emergency plan.

Physical:

1. Get extra sleep
    - Take a nap (napping when everybody is out of the house works best for me – I love it).
    - Plan to go to bed earlier or wake up later.
    - Cancel some plans so I can sleep in.
2. Physical exercise
    - Bike riding
    - Workout

- Basketball
- Racquetball
- Going for a walk

3. Get a massage.
4. Treat myself in some way (this doesn't sound very macho, but I've had a pedicure before and it is awesome).
5. Give myself permission for an extra long shower or a bath, especially with some Epsom salts if I'm really sore.

Emotional

1. Talk to my psychologist.
2. Talk to any of my support people.
3. Journal (increase the number of times and the amount that I normally journal).
4. Reach out to friends and plan something fun.

Intellectual

1. Read a novel (something by an author I enjoy or look for something totally new).
2. Learn a new skill (usually something physical like Aikido skills, or karate, but I've also started to mess around with musical instruments).
3. Read about an area that interests me (I like reading about things like quantum physics, chaos theory, and astrophysics – it excites me and makes me feel happy).
4. Watch documentaries.

Spiritual

1. Meditate.
2. Practice affirmative prayer.
3. Talk to my own spiritual adviser (I'll make an appointment and see if I can speak with her a little sooner than my regular appointment).

Financial

1. Talk to my financial adviser.
2. Look at my bank account.
3. Create a plan.
4. Discuss a plan with somebody I trust.

Social

1. Go out with friends.
2. Connect.
3. Talk to my wife.
4. Have a date night or weekend away with my wife.
5. Watch a movie.
6. Go driving and look at houses or drive in the country and talk with my wife.

Purpose

1. Ask myself, "What are you here for?"
2. Ask myself, "Why are you doing what you're doing in your life?"

Get more bang for your buck

Journaling hits the Purpose, Spiritual, Emotional, and Intellectual factors for me, so I can do one thing and hit them all. Team sports, like playing basketball with my friends, hits Social, Physical, and Intellectual, especially if I am learning new skills in the process.

Anything that's going to feed you with joy, soothe your body, and calm your nervous system – those are things I prioritize in my emergency plan.

The Me Factor System in Action

I use my Me Factor Owner's Manual as a guide. Just as with your car, if something starts to go wrong, consult the manual and figure out what you might need to do. Instead of an oil filter, you might need a relaxing walk. Instead of a tune-up, you might need a weekend with the guys.

One day I was driving on my daily commute to drop the kids off at school and then go to work. I knew I was tired and knew I was getting burned out, but I was doing what many men feel they're supposed to do – I was limping through it.

I shoulder-checked for traffic as I prepared to change lanes. I saw nothing, so I started to pull over when I heard the honk of a horn and quickly swerved back into my lane. As the driver I'd nearly hit gave me the finger, I realized, "Okay, that's enough." I dropped the kids off at school, canceled my day, and went home.

That day, I had a nice long nap. I had a bath. I took another nap. I watched some TV shows I had wanted to see. I went for a walk. I did things to take care of myself because I have learned that what I experienced in traffic is a late symptom. When basic items are falling through the cracks, you're no longer safe. This is why The Me Factor Owner's Manual is so important.

Realistically, if you're feeling very low on the Ten-Point Scale, you need some professional help. Talk to somebody. Talk to your doctor to start with and see if he or she can refer you to a good psychologist. Many people have health benefits through their employment, yet they don't realize they have coverage for psychological services. You might be pleasantly surprised to find out what's covered on your healthcare plan; even if you do have to pay for your visit, you will often be reimbursed for some, if not all, of the cost. There may even be free/low cost services, and it's worth the investment in yourself if you have the means to pay for it yourself.

If you drop to the level of a one or a two on the Ten-Point Scale, it's important to get help right away. You don't have to do this by yourself. You can't! A drowning man can't rescue himself. You have no leverage. This whole idea of pulling yourself up by your own bootstraps defies physics. It doesn't work.

What you can do is take small steps. Start small. You might not be able to pack up and head off into the mountains any time you start feeling low, but you may be able to take a five-minute break, sit quietly somewhere, and just breathe. You might be able to get yourself some food that you like – and take the time to enjoy it, as opposed to just scarfing it down so you can get back to work. Instead of jumping out of bed in the morning and hitting the ground running, you might get up three minutes earlier and take your time getting out of bed. Little steps can make a huge difference in pulling yourself out of a nosedive.

The Most Important Question You Can Ask

I've already mentioned the power of stopping to simply ask "Is this working for me?" This concept bears repeating because it applies to so many areas of life. You could ask that about what you're eating for lunch. You could ask it about the pair of shoes you're going to buy. Jobs, relationships, thoughts (especially thoughts and emotional reactions!!!) – all of these would benefit from an honest answer. If something isn't working for you, fix it! And if you can't fix it, get the hell away from it. Don't keep it in your life.

Personally, I've had to ask that question about my thought process plenty of times. I've asked it about relationships and jobs. The job I had that led me to that fearful morning in a motel in Lac La Biche was another time where I had to ask myself, "Is this working?" and, even more importantly, I had to acknowledge that it wasn't. I needed to do something different.

You have to ask yourself that question and have the courage to answer honestly and *act* when changes need to be made.

You Have a Choice

The problem that most people have – the problem that made me wake up one morning so burned out that I thought I was having a stroke – is that we don't always think we have a choice. We go along with life, putting one foot in front of the other, focusing on whatever happens to be screaming at us at the moment. When an issue can no longer be ignored, we address it and keep going. We never really take the time to sit and think about life in a proactive, deliberate way.

Making decisions based on feeding your goose and following The Me Factors is the one way to make sure you are choosing what is important for your life and understanding how your Me Factors fit together to give you the best outcome.

Conclusion

Where Do You Go from Here?

You are now well on your way to implementing your Me Factor System to get what the hell you want out of life. So, what happens next?

First off, be prepared: If you start implementing everything in this book all at once, your life is going to be chaotic for a while. That's okay. We all have a certain level of organization in our lives. It may not be ideal, but it's what we're comfortable with, so it's very easy to stay at that level. If you want to change, things have to go into chaos – a bit of flux. This can sometimes be overwhelming and unsettling, but if you keep going, it settles down and reorganizes itself at a higher order of complexity. It gets better, but you have to go through the tough adjustment phase first.

Think about cleaning out your garage. At the beginning of the process, it's probably not so bad. You move the little pieces of junk out of the way first so you can get to the big stuff. Halfway through, it's probably really chaotic. You're lugging big things around, trying to find space, and before you know it, it's a mess.

Here is the key: Keep going.

Too many people give up in the middle of the chaos because it just seems endless or they don't feel like finishing or are too intimidated by the mess. But in the end, you have a floor so clean you can eat off it. You can have your guys over to drink beer while you watch the game. You just have to get through that chaotic middle part in order to get to the good part. Don't be afraid of the chaos you are creating in your life from making these changes.

Any time you make a change, you get change back. I mentioned this at the beginning of the book. You get this in the form of "change back" messages from the people around you. When you start setting boundaries, looking after yourself, and making decisions that make sense to you, the people in your life are not necessarily going to like it – not because they don't like you but because they don't like change. That's human nature. Your friends, family, and coworkers know the old you, so they will expect you to *be* the old you. They will push back at the change. This is the normal process of change. Be prepared for that as you embark on your journey.

Not only will some relationships change, but some may have to end. Even though this can be tough, any relationships that do end are creating room for new ones to show up in your life, with people who actually like what you are offering and see you for who you really are.

Be Your Own Coach

Now that you have your Me Factor System, you have your own Owner's Manual for your life. You know how you work, you know what keeps you happy, and you get to be your own mentor and coach.

This process is not for the weak of heart. It takes guts to be in charge of your own life and to change the way you have been doing things. I suggest if you are ready to change, sit down with your family and say, "Hey, listen. I realize this is how we've been playing the game so far. But we need to change the rules. How do you guys feel about that?"

For most of us, our parents, mentors, and coaches had our best interests at heart, but they were also human. They were trying to do the best they could and were far from perfect. Our parents made mistakes and did things that they maybe should not have done. Or maybe they *didn't* do things they *should* have done.

Now, you have a chance to do things differently. It's time to "re-parent" yourself. Or maybe it's more accurate to call it "coach yourself." You can use the information in this book to come up with your own strategy for becoming your own mentor.

In your duties as your own coach, you'll have to make sure you get to bed at a regular time on a regular basis. Give yourself sabbaticals every so often. Eat right. Connect with good friends. Look after your financial health. Take time for spiritual enrichment. Do things that spark your brain to grow. These are the things our parents and mentors tried for years to teach us. Now we get to take matters into our own hands.

"You're Dropping Your Shoulder"

While you are reading this, you might be thinking this is going to take a lot of discipline or that it's going to be hard. As authors Gary Keller and Jay Papasan of *The ONE Thing* share, you only need discipline long enough to build the habit. Definitely use discipline up front, but it only takes three months to build solid habits. Then it gets easier.

Once you build a good self-coaching habit by using the tools in this book, your life will begin to flow. You have reprogrammed your autopilot. Tweak it, and keep expanding and fine-tuning it. It's far easier to live that way than to try to figure it out every day and keep asking yourself, "Well, what time should I go to bed today? Should I eat nutritiously today? Whom do I talk to today?" Have a plan and create a structure for yourself.

You're not fixing something that is broken. You are a work of Perpetually Evolving Perfection. You are filling in a deficit that you may not have identified before. No one told you how you should have been operating or you just realized that you could be doing better in a certain area.

Let's say you hire a golf coach to improve your game. Maybe you're having trouble with your drive, or you just want to see how you might do better. The pro can take one look at your swing and say, "There's the problem. You're dropping your shoulder." Self-evaluating – understanding what you are currently doing and how it could be better – is the first step to helping you make up that deficit. That's how you tell where you're "dropping your shoulder" and how to fill in whatever is missing.

Find More Help

If you have benefited from reading this book and are considering seeking more professional help, you might be wondering where to go next. Talking to a professional or a coach is an excellent next step because we don't always have objectivity for our own situations.

Having someone who has your back is a healthy thing. Tiger Woods has a golfing coach. Michael Jordan had a basketball coach. Just because they are among the best who have ever played in their respective sports does not mean they don't need help.

I have already outlined the difference between psychologists, psychiatrists, and clinical social workers. Registered clinical social workers are trained to provide therapy. Psychiatrists and psychologists will often work together to complete the puzzle; the psychiatrist will do the medication piece, and the psychologist will do the therapy piece.

All three professionals may be good choices for you. They all can do individual work or work with couples, families, or groups. The right choice may depend on what an individual happens to specialize in and how you feel in and about the relationship.

That said; don't be afraid to shop around. Ask about the following:

1. **Education.** Typically, a registered clinical social worker has a master's degree. Some clinical social workers have PhDs, but that is very rare. Most psychologists have PhDs or some sort of doctorate. Psychiatrists can't even call themselves a psychiatrist without a doctorate in medicine.
2. **Experience.** How long have they been practicing? Have they worked with people like you before? How often do they work with clients who have concerns similar to yours?
3. **Comfort level.** This is the most important question to ask yourself: Do you feel comfortable with this person? Therapy is very intimate, even in a group setting. Just like there are good plumbers and carpenters and crappy plumbers and carpenters, the same goes for psychologists and psychiatrists. Make sure you feel safe, that they act ethically, and that you are comfortable with them.

You Are the Goose

You now understand the importance of personal maintenance. You are the goose. You produce the golden eggs. If something happens to you, all the eggs you could have produced disappear. Looking after your kids, being successful at your job, having a strong, healthy relationship, contributing to the charities you care about – all of that stops if you fail to take care of yourself first.

I'll leave you with one very important step. Get a piece of paper and write out everything you have accomplished in your life – everything you can remember. I call it "My Greatest Hits List." As you write each thing out, assign it a number.

Once you have finished your list, look at it and pretend it isn't yours. Pretend it belongs to someone else. What would you think about this person and their "Greatest Hits"? You might be pleasantly surprised by how this shifts your perspective. You might even find yourself saying, "Wow, this person has done a lot of stuff." "They really got it going on." Then you'll realize, "Hey, wait a second, that's me! Maybe I'm not doing so bad after all."

My Greatest Hits List

1. ....
2. ....
3. ....
4. ....
5. ....
6. ....
7. ....
8. ....
9. ....
10. ....

Whenever you need to be in an empowered state of mind, review your Greatest Hits. Read it over and over again. Recite it to yourself. It will put you in the right state of mind to be successful. Keep adding to it. You'll find that as you do this your brain is getting trained to look for more stuff to put on your list – then your life feels like just one big positive vortex of success!

Your #1 priority now is to look after yourself.

Pour energy into the center of your Me Factor Schematic first, and the circles of your life will barely be able to contain the abundance that overflows.

Your life is *getting better*. You're not doing this because you are broken. You're doing this because you are already perfect where you are, and you are committed to getting even better.

Invest in yourself. You are the adventure! And you've just taken your first step on an expedition toward living life from a place of abundance and unlimited energy.

Now let's go out and get what the hell we want.

Now that you've been introduced to The Me Factor System go to go to TheMeFactor.me and sign up for my FREE Master Class. Ask me your burning questions so you can get even more of what the HELL you want.

About the Author

Dr. Ganz Ferrance is an International speaker, author, entrepreneur, and award-winning psychologist. He holds a PhD in Counseling Psychology and an MA in Developmental Psychology from Andrews University in Michigan. He is the former Public Education Coordinator and Vice-President of the Psychologists Association of Alberta. For over twenty-five years, Dr. Ferrance has been helping individuals, couples, families, and corporations reduce their levels of stress, improve their relationships, and enjoy more success.

"Dr. Ganz" is a favorite of the media, and over the past fourteen years has been interviewed by *The Edmonton Journal*, CBC Radio, 630 CHED, *Good Morning Canada*, *CTV News*, *Psychology Today*, *Ebony* magazine, Bloomberg Business Radio Network, and many other media outlets. He holds the John C. Patterson Media Award from the Psychologists' Association of Alberta and the Rosalina Smith Award from the National Black Coalition of Canada for Exceptional and Prolonged Service from an Individual from the Black Community Conducting a Business.

Dr. Ferrance's deep belief in "positive psychology" helps you be the best version of yourself. He presents his information in a straightforward, down-to-earth, no-nonsense way. He prides himself on being a fellow "work-in-progress" and does not present anything that he has not personally put his blood, sweat, and tears into. This approach has made him a sought-after public speaker – with audiences in the United States and Canada enjoying his fun, engaging, and life-changing presentations on beating stress and building superior relationships.

Dr. Ferrance has a black belt in karate and is currently studying Aikido. He lives in Edmonton, Alberta, Canada with his wife and two children.

References & Citations

[1] http://www.apa.org/monitor/oct01/multitask.aspx

[2] http://www.apa.org/news/press/releases/2015/02/money-stress.aspx

[3] https://www.psychologytoday.com/articles/200307/the-dangers-loneliness

[4] https://www.nytimes.com/2018/01/17/world/europe/uk-britain-loneliness.html

[5] https://www.newyorker.com/culture/cultural-comment/suicide-crime-loneliness

[6] http://bjsm.bmj.com/content/early/2017/03/30/bjsports-2016-096587

[7] https://sleepfoundation.org/press-release/national-sleep-foundation-recommends-new-sleep-times

[8] https://www.cnn.com/2016/12/06/health/sleep-driving-crash-risk/index.html

[9] http://time.com/3657434/night-work-early-death/

[10] http://www.huffingtonpost.ca/entry/your-body-does-incredible_n_4914577

[11] https://www.health.harvard.edu/blog/regular-exercise-changes-brain-improve-memory-thinking-skills-201404097110

[12] http://www.telegraph.co.uk/news/health/news/11337704/Playing-a-musical-instrument-may-lower-dementia-risk.html

[13] https://journal.thriveglobal.com/will-technology-ruin-your-childrens-development-663351c76974

[14] http://www.apa.org/news/press/releases/2017/11/lowest-point.aspx

[15] http://www.abfnet.org/